a world
to win

a world to win

to win

Essays on THE COMMUNIST MANIFESTO

Edited by PRAKASH KARAT

First published March 1999
Second edition July 1999

LeftWord Books
12 Rajendra Prasad Road, New Delhi 110 001, India
Phone: (91-11) 335 9456
Email: <leftword@vsnl.com> <LeftWord@hotmail.com>

LeftWord Books *is a division of Naya Rasta Publishers Pvt. Ltd.*
27–29 Bhai Vir Singh Marg, New Delhi 110 001, India

Manifesto of the Communist Party *first published in German 1848.*
This translation first published 1888.

ISBN 81-87496-00-2 (hardback)
ISBN 81-87496-01-0 (paperback)

Typeset in Minion and Frutiger

Printed at Progressive Printers
A 21, Jhilmil Industrial Area, G.T. Road, Shahdara, Delhi 110 095

For
E.M.S. NAMBOODIRIPAD

Contents

Note on the Text of
The Communist Manifesto

The text of

The Communist Manifesto that has been reprinted in this volume was translated by Samuel Moore in 1888 and edited by Engels, and is taken from the *Collected Works of Marx and Engels*, Moscow 1976, volume 6. The text of the 'Preface to the English Edition of 1888' was also translated by Moore and revised by Engels, and has been reprinted from the *Collected Works of Marx and Engels*, Moscow 1976, volume 26. The asterisked notes [*] in both the texts are by Engels, and are identified as such. The numbered notes are by the editors of the *Collected Works*.

Prakash Karat

Introduction

I

This book on *The Communist Manifesto* comes at the conclusion of the year marking its one hundred and fiftieth anniversary. The world-wide observance of the anniversary from February 1998 became an occasion for reappraising the historic significance of this remarkable document; for critically examining the contemporary state of Marxist theory; and for exploring new directions for the working class movement as we approach the twenty-first century.

The *Manifesto* was the first programmatic statement of the Communist movement. In the evolution of the thought of Marx and Engels, it was an exposition of the theory of historical materialism in a developed form. Lenin summed up its significance:

With the clarity and brilliance of genius, this work outlines a new world-conception, consistent materialism, which also embraces the realm of social life; dialectics, as the most comprehensive and profound doctrine of development; the theory of the class struggle and of the world-historic revolutionary role of the proletariat – the creator of a new, communist society.[1]

The *Manifesto* is a revolutionary charter for the anti-capitalist revolution: it equips the working class and other oppressed sections of society with the alternative vision of a socialist and Communist society. Unlike the earlier programmes of utopian and petty-bourgeois socialism, the *Manifesto* sets out the path to overthrow capitalism and realize socialism based on the actual conditions of society and historical development. The *Manifesto* places the working class in the central role, as the only revolutionary class which can act as the 'grave diggers' of the bourgeoisie. It declares that the proletariat 'can no longer emancipate itself' without 'freeing the whole of society from exploitation'.

The enduring vitality of the *Manifesto* is due to the power of scientific theory combined with the fundamental of strategy for a revolutionary movement. Complex theory has been expressed in a lucid and compressed manner making it intelligible to the ordinary worker. The *Manifesto* remains the most powerful piece of writing produced by the Communist movement.

The *Manifesto* belongs to that historical period which began with the French workers revolt in February. Two decades after this abortive revolution, the working people of Paris set up the Paris Commune in 1871 for a short period of time. Between these two historical landmarks of the working class movement, Marx and Engels gave the theory of scientific socialism a finished form. *Capital* (Volume 1) appeared in 1867 marking the mature analysis of capitalism. The period saw the setting up of the International Association of Working Men in 1864 and the rapid development of the ideas of Marx and Engels on organizing the proletariat as a class conscious force. It also saw

[1] V.I. Lenin, *Collected Works*, 21, p. 48

their increasing attention to the colonies, including India, which barely find reference in the *Manifesto*.

After the defeat of the Paris Commune, Marx and Engels looked towards Russia for the next revolutionary wave. In their joint preface to the Russian edition of the *Manifesto* in 1882, they point to a Russian revolution as 'the signal for the proletarian revolution in the West'.

The elaboration of the concept of imperialism by Lenin represented a major advance in the theory of the development of capitalism. It is what Prabhat Patnaik, in his essay in this book, calls 'the second peak' of unified theory which set the stage for the 1917 Russian revolution. The message of the *Manifesto* truly became a worldwide one riding the currents unleashed by the epoch-making event in Russia.

When the hundredth anniversary of the *Manifesto* was observed in 1948, the world was a different place. After heroic sacrifices, the Soviet Union had been instrumental in the defeat of fascism; the world was poised to witness the success of the Chinese revolution and the advance of the Vietnamese and Korean revolutions. The setting up of 'people's democracies' in Eastern Europe and the wave of national liberation movements were all part of the historic changes in the post-Second World War era. The end of the socialist experiment in the Soviet Union marked the close of this epoch. By the end of the eighties, the entire course of progressive developments came to be halted with the onset of a world-wide reaction. Marxism was faced with the greatest challenge to its existence and viability both in the theoretical and practical–political plane.

The seven years since the fall of the Soviet Union have witnessed sustained propaganda by imperialist circles and their ideologues about the death of socialism and the obsoleteness of Marxism. This ideological blitz has been accompanied by the most determined drive of international finance capital to reinforce its sway and to penetrate every area in the world. What is termed 'globalization' has constituted the most serious attack on the working people of both the developed and developing capitalist countries. The twin impact of these adverse events has seen the culmination of the process whereby some Communist parties have wilted and given up Marxism as a guiding theory.

At such a juncture, the one hundred and fiftieth anniversary of the *Manifesto* could well have been, at best, the commemoration of a historical document which has little contemporary value, or an occasion for a post-mortem of what went wrong with the seminal text on scientific socialism. Instead, the focus has been on the vulnerabilities of world capitalism and the striking relevance of Marx's analysis of the globalized capitalist system. 1998 saw the spreading crisis which began with South-East Asia's financial collapse; it soon extended to the East Asian region with South Korea stricken, and Japan, the second most powerful economy in the world, being plunged into financial difficulties and recession. The economic collapse of Russia and the instability in Brazil followed suit.

The mood of triumphalism evaporated in the face of this gloomy picture. Doubts and recriminations surfaced among the most ardent advocates of globalization about the policies being pursued by the IMF. 'The policy backlash is the most serious challenge yet to the free-market orthodoxy that the globe has embraced since the end of the Cold War' stated the *Wall Street Journal*.[2] Conversely, working class struggles were imbued with a new vigour from the mid-nineties. After the prolonged assault in the trade union movement in the advanced capitalist countries, the French workers strike of 1995 marked a turning point for the steadily gathering current of working class resistance.

The 150th anniversary of the *Manifesto* took place in this background. Hundreds of meetings, discussions and demonstrations were held. A notable event was the May 1998 conference in Paris which attracted 1500 participants from parties, trade unions, social movements and institutions, and more than 300 papers were published. It is not possible here to go over the entire range of material produced in these exercises. At the end of February 1999, when we scan the tenor and content of the discussions at the various conferences, meetings, and seminars, a notable feature is the shedding of any traces of despondency which affected the practitioners of Marxism since 1991.

---

[2] *Wall Street Journal*, quoted in Robert Wade and Frank Veneroso, 'The Battle Over Capital Controls', *New Left Review*, 231, 4 September 1998.

While introspection was a basic theme, there was also growing confidence for theoretical renewal and practical direction.

In order to reflect some of the discussions and intellectual work done in India during this anniversary, we asked three prominent Marxist scholars to contribute to this volume. Their three essays are framed by the concern for (a) locating the Manifesto in the thought of Marx and Engels; (b) its significance for Marxist theory; and (c) its role as guide to theory and action in the future. Irfan Habib sets out the understanding of history contained in the *Manifesto* and its subsequent development; Prabhat Patnaik stresses the need for 'reconstituting Marxist theory' to scale new heights. For this he analyses the new developments in the contemporary world economy which have to be properly addressed. Aijaz Ahmad provides a cogent overview of the complex revolutionary ideas expressed in the *Manifesto* and assesses their impact in the realm of the economic structure and the attendant sphere of politics and culture.

All three thoughtful essays point out the inadequate treatment of colonialism in the theory of capitalist development worked out by Marx upto the first volume of *Capital* which he completed. The contributions in this book have not dealt with the question of assimilating the experience of building socialism in the Soviet Union which is a necessary part of reviewing and revitalizing Marxist theory and practice. This needs separate and elaborate attention.

II

The capitalism that the *Manifesto* describes has a startling contemporaneity – a feature noted by both Marxists and non-Marxists. The 'globalized capitalism' existing in the late twentieth century was envisaged with brilliant clarity in the passages dealing with the spread of capitalist relations in the *Manifesto*: 'The need of a constantly expanding market for its products chases the bourgeoisie over the whole surface of the globe. It must nestle everywhere, settle everywhere, establish connexions everywhere.'

While the analysis of capitalism was not complete in the 1848 work, it progresses and assumes a mature form in *Capital*. Subsequently Lenin's *Imperialism* opened the way for new initiatives for the Communist movement. The developments within the imperialist structure since then, particularly the growth of speculative international finance capital in the last two decades of this century, is a major concern for Marxist theory and for working class movements around the globe.

A specific problem thrown up by the situation is the role of the nation-state in the globalized imperialist system which has direct implications for the class struggle. There has been an erosion of the sovereignty of nation-states due to their inability to exercise regulatory functions when faced with the volatility and demands of speculative finance capital that moves with impunity across borders. The nature of this type of finance capital and its phenomenal growth need not detain us here. But it is important to recognize the enormous difficulties such flows of finance capital cause for nation-states, which are unable to prevent its predatory inroads or to counter the policies it imposes through the IMF–World Bank combine and the World Trade Organization. The question is whether these harmful trends can be fought through the medium of the nation-state and by making the nation-state the centrepiece for class struggles.

For this, a proper appreciation of the nation-state as the arena of class struggle is required. The *Manifesto*, which outlines the global character of capitalist operations, at the same time emphasizes the importance of class struggle within national boundaries: 'Though not in substance, yet in form, the struggle of the proletariat with the bourgeoisie is at first a national struggle. The proletariat of each country must, of course, first of all settle matters with its own bourgeoisie.' One hundred and fifty years later, this principle is still valid, despite the vastly increased internationalization of capital.

In this context, it is important to understand the role of the ruling classes in the lesser-developed capitalist countries. The bourgeois–landlord classes in most of these countries have abandoned the quest for a relatively autonomous development of capitalism within their countries and embraced free-market prescriptions. The integration with the global order of international finance capital is seen as the only path for their class development in a world in which the Soviet Union is absent as a countervailing force. This, however, cannot be a permanent phenomenon. As the contradictions in the world capitalist system intensify, there will be shifts in the positions of the domestic ruling classes.

The vulnerability of these nation-states in the face of international capital flows is substantial, but it should not be exaggerated to the point of helplessness. The orthodoxy of the IMF–World Bank postulates that no country can survive and develop without opening up to free capital flows. But the South-East Asian crisis illustrates, above all, the folly of such unregulated capital flows. It also illustrates that the nation-state is the only instrument available to regulate the depredations of finance capital and to put this on the agenda of international forums. For example, despite the Mahathir regime being unabashedly capitalist, Malaysia challenged this Fund–Bank orthodoxy by imposing capital controls.

The nation-state and its mechanisms cannot be left to be wielded by the domestic ruling classes to implement the dictates of international finance.[3] Both for the immediate protection of the working people and the fight against imperialist domination, the struggle to reorient the direction of the state must be waged with determination. The working class movement must take the leadership of the entire people in this struggle. This is what is implied in the *Manifesto* which exhorts the working class to 'rise to be the leading class of the nation' and 'constitute itself the nation', if it is to acquire political supremacy. The increasing weight of the working class-led democratic movement against imperialist subjugation would bring about a shift in the national correlation of forces and open the way to check and counter the pro-imperialist shift of the domestic ruling classes.

The class struggle will be conducted mainly in the terrain of the nation-state; this is not a negation of internationalism. The imperialism of today aggressively seeks to suborn the nation-state to enforce its policies rather than allow the state to act on the priorities of the domestic classes and the people. Loss of sovereignty of the nation translates directly into loss of sovereignty for the people and their rights. The sovereignty of the people is expressed through democratic

---

[3] Both Prabhat Patnaik and Aijaz Ahmad have written about the nation-state and globalization. See Patnaik, 'Globalization of Capital and the Theory of Imperialism', *Social Scientist* 282–83, November–December 1996, and Ahmad, 'Globalization and the Nation-State', *Seminar* 437, January 1996.

institutions that represent nation-states and their people. The erosion of sovereignty is not in economic terms alone, it undermines political institutions and democracy, and affects people's rights in public education, health and social security.

The issue in India is precisely this at present. Among the Third World countries, India has a relatively more developed bourgeoisie and a republican constitution which underpins a defective but functioning parliamentary democracy. The 'globalization' agenda which has been embraced by the Indian ruling classes in the 1990s has opened the way for a direct attack on this form of democracy.

In India, there has always been the divorce between the political system with democratic forms and the economic structure which is grossly unequal and authoritarian, which is typical of the advanced capitalist countries.[4] But within this framework another dichotomy between the popular mandate and governmental decision-making has emerged. Regardless of which bourgeois party comes to power, it proceeds to implement the very same basic economic policies. This has been the record of three successive governments consisting of different political formations after 1991. The prevailing consensus amongst ruling class parties in Third World countries is a formidable obstacle in reversing the gamut of policies of neo-liberalism and the roll-back of the state.

While it is axiomatic that the Left refuses to be co-opted in this consensus and continues to build resistance to imperialist pressures, the real alternative cannot be presented in terms of economic policy changes alone. They are crucial but not sufficient. The fight for sovereignty, for democracy and the unity of the people has to have a political–ideological component. For, as the *Manifesto* underlines, 'the class struggle is essentially a political struggle'. The advance of Marxist theory and practice in the Third World countries depends on how effectively we tackle this conjuncture of class struggle in a nation-state with a dominant imperialist–globalized system.

---

[4] Ellen Meiksins Wood has highlighted this aspect of separation of the political and the economic under capitalism. See her *Democracy Against Capitalism: Renewing Historical Materialism,* Cambridge 1995.

The *Manifesto*, while correctly foreseeing the triumphant ascendancy of global capitalism, was over-optimistic about its capacity to break-down national barriers. 'National differences and antagonisms between the peoples are daily more and more vanishing, owing to the development of the bourgeoisie, to freedom of commerce, to the world market, to uniformity in the mode of production . . .'. In the era of imperialism, the twentieth century witnessed two world wars originating in imperialist-driven national rivalries and a host of national conflicts leading to mass slaughter. Evidently the rise of bourgeois rule exacerbates national rivalries and its effects carry on even in states which transit from capitalism.

At present, the struggle against imperialism is impeded and complicated by a host of ethnic–nationality–religious problems in the Third World countries and the former socialist states. The implantation of free-market principles, the retreat of socialist influence, and the impact of the destructive force of globalization in the social and cultural spheres have stimulated or aggravated ethnic religious identities and feelings. The rise of religious sectarian movements and ethnic–caste conflicts is a reactionary response to current crises faced by nation-states and multinational states in all parts of the world. Imperialism has the capacity to accommodate and co-opt such forces. US imperialism in South Asia is capable of collaborating with the Taliban in Afghanistan, the Islamic fundamentalist forces in Pakistan and the Hindu chauvinists in India. The disruption of popular unity, due to the chauvinist and undemocratic attitude of the ruling classes towards the minorities and because of the rise of sectarian forces often backed by imperialism, has to be countered by the working class movement and the Left.

The Left cannot aspire for national hegemony unless it doggedly builds a democratic movement which incorporates and guarantees the rights of ethnic and religious minorities. Countering both the 'big' and 'little' chauvinisms is required if the working class has to head an anti-imperialist nationalism. The experience of the South Asian countries should lead to more emphasis by the Left on federalism and regional autonomy as one of the ways to meet the democratic aspirations of the minorities and to counter separatism. Further, the struggle for democratic rights for the people is now partly reflected in the struggle for decentralization of decision-making powers in the administrative and economic spheres.

The break-up of the multinational states of the Soviet Union and Yugoslavia makes it all the more imperative to take a fresh look at Marxist theory and practice in this sphere.

IV

All efforts to negate the message of the *Manifesto* focus on the centrality accorded to the working class in the revolutionary transformation of society. The reverses suffered by socialism in the last decade have only reinforced the trend which seeks to revise this part of Marxist theory. Contrary to this revisionism, the recent experience of the struggle against globalization provides adequate ground to assert the central role of the working class. It is only this class which has offered consistent resistance to the imperialist offensive, however defensive it may have been. The French workers strike of 1995, the heroic month-long general strike of the South Korean workers in 1996, and the new, incipient forms of coordinated trade union struggles developing in Western Europe against the European Union's pro-big business policies confirm the pivotal role workers will play in the coming days.

As Aijaz Ahmad points out in his essay, the working class today is neither disappearing nor shrinking in size. This is true of even the advanced capitalist countries.[5] But the composition and internal structure of the work-force has changed. In India, the differentiation on caste and ethnic lines persists in the consciousness of workers. Very little attention has been paid to the formation of class consciousness by ideological and cultural intervention to supplement the political–organizational activities. Apart from this, what is of great import for the trade unions and the working class movement in general is the role of women workers. The *Manifesto* envisaged the growing induction of women into the industrial work force. 'The more modern in-

---

[5] 'In the industrial [OECD] nations of the North as a whole, there were 115 million people employed in "industry" in 1994 compared with 112 million in 1973'. Kim Moody, *Workers in a Lean World*, London 1997.

dustry becomes developed, the more is the labour of men superseded by that of women'. Women would become part of the growing proletariat as a cheap source of labour power. At the end of the twentieth century women constitute an average of 60 per cent of the work force in the advanced capitalist countries.[6] More and more women are employed predominantly in the service sector and in part-time and contract work with low wages. The same phenomenon is seen in the developing countries. In India, the female labour force amounts to 127 million. There is insufficient recognition that they are a vital part of the proletariat. Besides, it is necessary that the working class party take up the gender-specific issues of proletarian women along with the class exploitation they face. Without women workers being an integral part of the movement, the *Manifesto's* aim of the immense majority led by the working class winning the 'battle for democracy' is inconceivable.

The *Manifesto* was written for the Communist League, a party of German workers, albeit a small one. It therefore deals with the strategy and tactics that Communists should adopt, which presages the future methods adopted by the Communist movement. The *Manifesto* also explains the need for the working class to become organized into a party. 'This organization of the proletarians into a class, and consequently into a political party' is the embryonic idea which Lenin later developed into the full-fledged concept of a revolutionary party. Unlike what some claim, the idea of a vanguard is inherent in the *Manifesto's* conception of the role of Communists who are 'the most advanced and resolute of the working class parties of every country'. At the same time, Marx and Engels envisaged a number of working class parties and drew a basic distinction between parties of the propertied classes and parties of the working class.[7]

---

[6] The proportion of women between 15 and 64 years of age in the labour force in OECD countries rose from 53 per cent in 1980 to 60 per cent in 1990. ILO, *World Employment Report*, 1994, p. 29.

[7] 'In its struggle against the collective power of the propertied classes, the working class cannot act as a class except by constituting itself into a political party, distinct from, and opposed to, all old political parties formed by the propertied classes.' Resolution of the General Congress of the International Working Men's Association held at The Hague, September 1872. Marx and Engels, *Collected Works*, 23, p. 243.

In order to lay the theoretical basis for such a revolutionary party, the third section of the *Manifesto* is solely devoted to refuting the false versions of socialism and their incompatibility with scientific socialism. It is a reminder of the constant necessity for ideological struggle against the many variants of 'socialism' which emerge in different historical periods which are representative of non-working class ideologies.

The last section in the *Manifesto* is on the position of the Communists in relation to other opposition parties in the various countries of Europe. It sets out the tactics to achieve the immediate aims of the working class – the tactics of united front. As tactics to meet the 'momentary interests' of the working class, they are to be discarded when the situation changes. Marx and Engels themselves pointed out in a preface to a later edition that such references to tactics had become outdated. The political part of the *Manifesto* on the role of the party, its relationship with the class, the nature of the bourgeois state, and the strategy and tactics of a revolutionary movement is a rich source of ideas which needs to be reflected upon and viewed in the context of the later development of parties and the Internationals. There are many questions about the party, the class, and the state which remain unresolved after the experience of the Soviet Union and the other socialist states set up in the twentieth century.

V

All the contributions in this book are concerned with Marxist theory and practice in general, though the Indian context constantly appears. The seven decades-old Communist movement in India has accumulated a rich repository of struggles and experience. They need to be studied and analyzed and theorized. Unlike many other countries, in the post-1991 era, India continues to have parties with mass bases adhering to Marxism. Membership in the Communist parties and groups number around 1.5 million. There are another 55 to 60 million members in class and mass organizations which are Left-oriented.

Compared to this influence, there is a neglect of theory and inadequate attention is paid to the resources which can go into strengthening theoretical work. One major weakness is the negligible interaction between Marxist writings in Indian languages, except through English. While preparing this book, it was found that there was no information on the history of the *Manifesto* in the major languages of the Indian subcontinent. Some of this information has been put together for the first time and it is appended as a note. From the 1920s, the *Manifesto* attracted the attention of some of the best Indian minds active in the anti-imperialist struggle and in social movements.

They range from Abul Kalam Azad, outstanding nationalist leader and Islamic scholar, and E.V. Ramaswamy Naicker, the foremost social reformer and pioneer of the Dravidian movement, to the future leaders of the Communist movement P. Sundarayya and E.M.S. Namboodiripad. All of them were involved in the translation or publication of the *Manifesto*. The diverse political backgrounds of these leaders shows the wide influence and impact of Marxist ideas during the freedom struggle.

It is a good augury that the LeftWord Books has been launched with the present volume on *The Communist Manifesto*. In the task of enlivening Marxist theory and practice, the *Manifesto* will always be of help to understand the 'line of march' that we have to adopt.

In early 1998, when this book was first conceived of, we had asked E.M.S. Namboodiripad to write the introduction for it. He had shown great interest in the idea and had agreed to write. But that was not to be; he died a few weeks later. This book is dedicated to his memory.

Aijaz Ahmad

The Communist Manifesto
In Its Own Time,
And In Ours

It is said

that the Bible and the Quran are the only two books that have been printed in more editions and disseminated more widely than *The Communist Manifesto*. This brief and terse text thus has a pre-eminent position in the entire history of secular literature. Some sense of the breadth of its influence can be gauged from the fact that some 544 editions are known to have been published in 35 languages – all of them European languages, one might add – even prior to the Bolshevik Revolution; there must have been during that same period other editions which are not known, and infinitely greater number of editions were to be published, in very many more languages, European and non-European, *after* the Revolution of 1917. It is worth emphasizing, furthermore, that, unlike the two religious books that are said to have had a wider circulation, the *Manifesto* is barely one hundred and fifty years old: rather a young text, all things considered. It is much too early to fully assess the influence this young little pamphlet has had in the past and is likely to have in the future.

One can also say without fear of refutation that the *Manifesto* has been more consequential in the actual making of the modern world than any other piece of political writing, be it Rousseau's *Social Contract*, the American Constitution and the Bill of Rights, or the French 'Declaration of the Rights of Man and the Citizen'. The first reason is of course the power of its political message which has reverberated throughout the world and determined the destinies of a large cross-section of humanity over the past one hundred and fifty years. Then there is the style itself: no call to arms has ever been phrased in a language of such zest, beauty and purity. Third, there is the stunning combination of diagnosis and prediction. Marx describes the capitalism of his own times and predicts its trajectories into the indefinite future with such force and accuracy that every subsequent generation, in various parts of the world, has seen in the *Manifesto* the image of its own times and premonition of the horrors yet to come. And, fourth, concealed in the direct simplicity of its prose, like the labour of the tailor that disappears into the coat,[1] is the *distillation* of a multifaceted philosophical understanding that had arisen out of a series of confrontations with the thinkers most influential in the Germany of his times: Hegel, Feuerbach, Proudhon, Stirner, Bruno Bauer, Sismondi, the 'True Socialists' and the all the rest whom the authors of the *Manifesto* broadly describe as 'would-be universal reformers'.[2]

---

[1] The vivid phrase, 'labour of the tailor that disappears into the coat', is from Louis Althusser who coined it in an entirely different context.

[2] *The Communist Manifesto* has always been published as the joint product of Marx and Engels. That is not entirely inaccurate. In the present essay, however, I refer punctually to Marx as the author of this text. This calls for some explanation. The simplest reason is a matter of stylistic convenience; it is easier to refer to one author than constantly refer to both of them. There is also the question of historical accuracy in the strict sense, on two counts. First, we *know* that the final draft was prepared by Marx alone, at a time when Engels was not available for consultation and the Communist League was threatening punitive action against 'Citizen Marx' for the delay; the responsibility was his and was perceived

Much of the richness of the *Manifesto* is owed to the fact that it is the text of an intellectual and political transition. Marx alone – and then, increasingly, Marx and Engels together – had written so very much before coming to draft the *Manifesto* that one now quite forgets how very young (not quite thirty years old) he really was. This is the first *mature* text of a very young man. So, it *concludes* certain lines of argument Marx had been developing previously – in his first significant text, *Critique of Hegel's Doctrine of the State* and 'A Contribution to the Critique of Hegel's Philosophy of Right: An Introduction'; and then in 'The Jewish Question', the *Economic and Philosophical Manuscripts* (also knows as 'Paris Manuscripts'), the famous 'Theses on Feuerbach', and *The German Ideology*. Of these, Marx published only the *Critique* and 'The Jewish Question' in his own lifetime; the rest were drafted mainly for self-clarification and were then 'abandoned' – in the famous self-ironical phrase about *The German Ideology* – 'to the gnawing criticism of mice'. These texts, together with *The Holy Family, The Poverty of Philosophy,* and a number of minor essays of that time serve both as a prelude to the formulations that are so familiar to us now from the *Manifesto,* but also as a series of confrontations with the most influential tendencies in the Philosophy, Economics and Political Thought that were central to the intellectual universe within which Marx had first learned to think. They are, in short, oppositional texts, texts in which Marx stutters and stammers,

to be as such. Second, any comparison between the text of the *Manifesto* with the two earlier texts, 'Draft of a Communist Confession of Faith' and 'Principles of Communism', which Engels had produced only a few months earlier, would show how very sweeping were Marx's departures from those preparatory materials. Quite aside from the radical revision of substance, virtually every sentence in the key first Part, 'Bourgeois and Proletarians', bears the inimitable signature of Marx's style, demonstrating, as was usual in his writing, that Marx was one of the great stylists in the history of nineteenth century prose. Engels' contribution to this text was substantive but more indirect, in the sense that the materialist conception of history which the text so pithily summarizes was developed by both of them together, notably in *The German Ideology.* Earlier versions of this conception are also to be found in such texts as *The Economic and Philosophical Manuscripts* which belong to Marx alone, and in *The Holy Family* which began as a 15-page pamphlet by Engels and which Marx then expanded into a whole book. As Engels himself always recognized, Marx was the senior partner in what they humourously called their 'joint firm'.

refuses other people's thoughts, tries to think his own thoughts and define his own premises, tries to come out from under the whole weight of that immensely powerful body of thought that has come down to us under the labels of the Enlightenment, post-Enlightenment, Romanticism, Anarchism, utopian socialism, not to speak of the discourse of Rights and the fetishization of the market and the State.

Those earlier texts include passages and entire sections of great originality. However, virtually all of them are written in opposition to some particular writers or tendencies, i.e., Hegel and the others we have mentioned above. This kind of focussed criticism is continued in the latter section of the *Manifesto* as well, but the memorable first part can be viewed as perhaps the first of Marx's texts that is written entirely in the declarative, in opposition to not this or that thinker, this or that tendency in thought, but in opposition to bourgeois society as a whole. It is a text written at the end of a difficult apprenticeship, so as to scatter the spectres that had haunted European thought until that time and to define a new kind of relationship between political economy, history and philosophy, with the ambition of *realizing* the aims of philosophy through a double movement. This double movement consisted, on the one hand, of a theory of history which makes concrete the intellectual project of philosophy by explaining the fundamental motion of the material world in its generality – what postmodernism these days dismisses as a 'modes of production narrative'. But, on the other hand, it also demanded from philosophy that its ethical project be materialized as the *praxis* of a revolutionary transformation of an ethically intolerable world – what postmodernism now dismisses as 'the myth of Progress'.

Marx's mature studies of the world economy in general, and of the principles of capitalist economy in particular, belong of course to the period after the composition of the *Manifesto*. The engagement had begun much earlier, however, as we see in the systematic and constantly improving expositions of the subject in *The Economic and Philosophical Manuscripts* and *The German Ideology* which he did not publish in his own lifetime, as well as *The Poverty of Philosophy* which he did. A principle that had struck him quite early was that the rate and quantum of historical change in the forces and relations of production was much quicker under capitalism, and tended to get even quicker in each successive phase, as compared to antecedent modes of production where changes in the relations of production remained relatively limited and the pace of technological change relatively very slow; not 'unchanging' as he sometimes hastily said, but on the whole glacially slow. As a fundamental methodological principle, then, Marx adopted the view that it is impossible to grasp the essence of capitalism if we were to study it as a static reality, or mainly as it quite evidently is at a given time. Rather, the pace of change within this mode of production required that it be studied as a *process*, whose past had to be understood historically and whose future trajectory could be deduced from its past and present with reasonable degree of accuracy, not in all details but in its overall structure. This explains why the picture that the *Manifesto* presents of capitalism tells us so little about how capitalism was in his own time, and tells much more of how it had been and how it was likely to unfold.

Even so, within the larger corpus of Marx's work the *Manifesto* cannot be regarded as a text of some final illumination. As was said above, it is a *transitional* text, the *first* mature text of a very young man. It not only transits from earlier texts but also gropes toward those more comprehensive studies that were to follow over the next many years. The range of that corpus is breathtaking. Three preoccupations were paramount in that whole range of work, however. There was, first, the effort to offer the most incisive, most detailed account of the capitalist mode of production as such: the first principles and the first premises for an account of the modern world as a whole, from the standpoint of labour, production and the struggle of classes. The massive *Grundrisse*, which too Marx drafted only for self-clarification, in 1857–58, and of course the three volumes of *Capital* and *Theories of Surplus Value* are the key texts of that historic project. Second, there was extensive engagement with the history and politics of his own time as these unfolded all around him; among numerous such texts, 'The Class Struggle in France', first published as a series of articles in 1850, and 'The Eighteenth Brumaire of Louis Bonaparte', composed two years later as yet another series of articles, are the most magisterial. Rarely, if ever, has journalism risen to such heights of analytic and theoretical grandeur. Finally, there are equally numerous writings of Marx as a militant of the labour movement, most famously the 'Critique of the Gotha Program' which he drafted almost thirty years after the *Manifesto*, in the wake of the experience of the Paris Commune and, thanks to that experience, directly concerned, in whatever preliminary fashion, with what a Communist society of the future may in broad outline strive to be. All three preoccupations of later life – the history and political economy of capitalism as a whole; contemporary politics of the ruling classes; the premises of the labour movement – are foreshadowed in the *Manifesto* itself. If it refines the general statement of the materialist conception of history as it had been defined up to *The German Ideology*, its thrust toward a theory of the political economy of capitalism would be immeasurably improved by the time Marx came to write *Capital*. It is on the basis of this whole edifice, with the *Manifesto* serving as a beam in the middle, that later masters of Marxism, such as Lenin and Rosa Luxemburg, were to make seminal contribution to the Marxist theory in general as well as to a fuller understanding of their own time, notably on the issue of imperialism and the actual strategy and tactics of the labour movement.

Approaches to the *Manifesto*

There are many ways of looking at the *Manifesto*. Each one of its significant propositions had received detailed, though sometimes less rigorous, treatment in the earlier texts and was to surface again, often in very much more precise and enriched forms, in later writings. The pithy characterization of the state executive as 'the managing committee of the whole bourgeoisie', for example, would be understood in a much more nuanced and dialectical fashion if we were to read it in the perspective of the far more detailed treatment of the subject in the earlier *Critique of Hegel's Doctrine of the State* and 'The Jewish Question' and the later, maturer 'The Eighteenth Brumaire'. Similarly, the cryptic comment on the nature of consciousness in Section Two – 'Does it require deep intuition to comprehend that man's ideas, views and conceptions, in one word, man's consciousness, changes with every change in the conditions of his material existence, in his social relations and in his social life' – can be usefully compared with the sharper formulation of twelve years later, in the 'Preface' to *The Critique of Political Economy*: 'It is not the consciousness of men that determines their existence, but, on the contrary, it is their social existence that determines their consciousness'. Indeed, this had been a constant theme in Marx's writing after he had developed his own critique of Hegel's idealism soon after finishing his university education. But our understanding of these very condensed formulations can be vastly enriched through a reading of *The German Ideology* where Marx makes the fundamental point that *all* consciousness is intrinsically class consciousness in the sense that all consciousness is *formed* within class society, from the moment of birth onward, so that one may have the consciousness of the class into which one is born or one may adopt the consciousness of some other class (e.g., a proletarian internalizing a consciousness propagated by the capitalist system) but there is no such thing as a *class-less consciousness*. Antonio Gramsci was to make much of this insight, for example, arguing that since one imbibes one's consciousness from different and conflicting segments of society, individual consciousness is necessarily a contradictory and incoherent consciousness which can be made coherent only through great effort of education, reflection and practical interaction with others who are comrades in the same struggle. A reading of this kind, where elements of the thought expressed in the *Manifesto* are systematically related to the more detailed exposition of those same elements in other, earlier and later texts of Marx, as well as to the thought of later Marxists, is perhaps the most fruitful way of approaching the *Manifesto*. In itself, individual sentences in the text can mislead as to what Marx thought on the subject.

Or, one can read the *Manifesto* as a text of its own time. For all its timeless grasp of the fundamental premises of capitalist society, it is also a text very much of its time, i.e. of the working class movement living with a great sense of urgency because all could see that a great revolutionary upheaval was fast approaching in which the proletariat would be necessarily involved, so that the correct political standpoint was a matter not only of the long future but of the very palpable present. And, indeed, the first edition of the *Manifesto* was published in London weeks before the revolution of 1848 broke out in Paris and spread like wildfire through what today would be known as thirteen different countries in Europe. It was expected, as undoubtedly happened, that the urban proletariat would provide the bulk of the revolutionary mass, and the *Manifesto* was very much a call for the international class *unity* and political self-organization and *autonomy* of the proletariat, across the diverse countries, in a way that the proletariat had not been united in independent action in the previous revolutionary upheavals. Programmatic statements like 'The Communists do not form a separate party opposed to other working class parties' would be opaque to today's reader without grasping that (a) the Communist League was so small an organization that an attempt to convert it into a political party in today's sense would have been futile and sectarian at best; (b) that the various segments of the working class were deeply fragmented along the ideological lines that are dealt with in Section III so that ideological struggle against those other tendencies was perceived as being a precondition for the subsequent formation of the 'party of the whole'; (c) that most European countries at the time had nothing resembling a constitutional, representative government, so that the unity not only of different sections of the politically active proletariat but also of what in Section IV are described as 'democratic parties' was seen as a precondition for a successful revolutionary offensive;[3] and (d) that the formulation is directly connected with the central emphasis on the unity of the class as a whole, which was then reflected with the call to arms with which the text concludes: 'Workers of the World, Unite!'[4]

---

[3] It is in this perspective that 'to win the battle of democracy' is seen as 'the first step in the revolution' for establishing 'the political supremacy of the working class'. Elsewhere, 'dictatorship of the proletariat' would itself be described as 'democracy carried to its fullest' and as the right of the majority to act in the interest of the majority. Since the majority is necessarily proletarianized under capitalism, and since democracy is conceived of as rule of the majority, Marx sometimes uses words 'proletarian' and 'democratic' to mean the same thing, and the phrase 'dictatorship of the proletariat' was initially designed to convey the same nuance. All of that is at least very confusing for today's reader but makes perfect sense when the standpoint is understood.

[4] As indicated partially in the previous note, the terminology of the *Manifesto* can pose many problems for the unwitting reader. In his famous commentary on the *Manifesto*, Ryazanoff points out that in the foreword to the original German edition of *The Condition of the Working Class in England*, Engels tells us that he makes use of words like worker, proletarian, working class, non-possessing class,

One could also read the *Manifesto*, especially Section I, purely from the philosophical point of view. It is well to recall that Marx's original training, and a very rigorous training at that, was in philosophy. He was deeply steeped in the thought of Spinoza, Kant, and Hegel, not to speak of scores of lesser philosophers such as Feurbach who had been at the time very influential among German youth, especially in contestation with the thought of Hegel. At every step in his philosophy of history Marx is engaged with various aspect of Hegel's thought. His conception of the proletarian consciousness as the 'true' consciousness, for example, is directly in line with the Master–Slave dialectic in Hegel's *Phenomenology* where Hegel argues that the slave always knows more about himself *as well as the Master*, hence about society as a whole, because he needs to know not only about himself but also the whole condition of his enslavement, including specially the character and conduct of the master, whereas the master need know nothing about the slave more than that the latter labours for him.

By contrast, Marx's theory of the state as inevitably the instrument of the ruling class is counterpoised directly against Hegel's view of the state as a superior, disinterested mechanism for reconciling antagonisms in civil society – indeed, Marx's theory of the State, which is stated so economically in the *Manifesto*, arose initially out of his

and proletariat to refer to the one and the same phenomenon. Some of that generalized sense of the word 'proletariat' is there in the *Manifesto* as well; much of what got called the 'Paris proletariat' then was comprised of the more pauperized craftsmen, struggling shopkeepers, and a variety of proletarianized urban clusters living as often by wit as by wage but overwhelmingly outside modern factory production. A further example refers to the much maligned formulation regarding 'the idiocy of rural life'. Hobsbawm points out that the original German word 'idiotismus' is much closer to the Greek 'idiotes' which has the meaning not of 'stupidity' or 'soft-headedness' but of 'narrow horizon' or 'isolation from wider society' and, more interestingly, 'a person concerned only with his own private affairs and not with those of the wider community'. The import of Marx's use of the word 'idiot' is thus closer to 'isolated' in one sense and 'individualist' in another. This, then, is connected with the crucial Marxist distinction between the individual character of peasant production and the collective character of the production of the industrial proletariat. There are numerous other misunderstandings of this kind, pertaining to our text, which are unfortunately much too common.

close, critical, passage-by-passage reading of Hegel when he was still a student. One could go even further and argue that it was his rejection of the Hegelian concept of the state as the highest form of social synthesis, and his theoretical discovery that the state exists not as a resolution of social conflicts but as a precise *expression* of those conflicts, which eventually led him to posit the theory of class struggle itself, i.e., the idea that class conflict is the most fundamental conflict in any society and that no state authority can be neutral in, or suspended above, this conflict. This Marx had first argued philosophically, while settling his accounts with Hegel, well before he set out to prove the thesis empirically, through a careful study of the laws of political economy.

In another direction, his sweeping denunciation of commerce as being a mechanism of conquest and exploitation of the dominated peoples and regions is counterposed directly against Kant's view of commerce as an instrument of peaceful exchange and friendship among nations. One could offer many more such examples of his engagements with philosophical masters of the past, in a wide range of philosophical discourses from political theory to ontology. The main point here, however, is that just as Marx was to later become a master of political economy essentially by formulating an unassailable critique of political economy, he was already launched, well before drafting the *Manifesto*, on a critique of philosophy so fundamental and extensive that Balibar, the contemporary French philosopher, has called it an 'anti-philosophy'.[5] Marx was determined, in other words, never to become a philosopher in the sense in which German Idealists, for example, were philosophers, even though so much of the language of *German Ideology* itself is imbued with the language of that idealism. One would want to add that this 'anti-philosophy' was possible precisely because of the extent to which he had mastered the philosophical discourse as such. Marx is in fact so deeply conversant with philosophical concepts – theory of consciousness, dialectics, the universal and the particular, and so on – and he uses them so casually that one does not quite feel the weight of philosophical thought that

[5] Etienne Balibar, *The Philosophy of Marx*, London 1995; French original, 1993.

undergirds the lightness and clarity of his prose. I have myself pub-lished an essay on his radically new way of employing and re-defining the concept of 'universality' in the *Manifesto* which simply overturns, on this particular subject, the whole legacy of eighteenth and nine-teenth century European philosophy.[6]

There are so many approaches to the *Manifesto* that if one were to adopt them all one could go on writing virtually indefinitely. My main concern throughout the present reflection on the text is to dem-onstrate, mainly by giving examples, how rich and complex and elu-sive a text this brief pamphlet really is. I have by and large refrained from commenting on the latter sections of the *Manifesto*, although those too are replete with surprises. A reflection on the varieties of 'reactionary socialism', and on 'utopian socialism', may at the end in fact bring us closer to some strands in the dominant Indian political discourse, including that of Gandhi who was himself deeply influ-enced by the utopian movement (though not by the specific utopians Marx discusses) and by conservative, right-wing critiques of capital-ism, as in Carlyle or Tolstoy or Ruskin. All that I have set aside, for lack of space. In the rest of this essay, I want to comment only on a few more issues at some length, which too shall bring up some related concerns: In what sense, and to what extent, is the bourgeoisie per-ceived to be revolutionary? And, what is the Marxist conception of the 'laws' of history? In his portrait of globalization as it was to unfold over time, does Marx give us an equally accurate picture of the capi-talist economy as well as the attendant political and aesthetic forms? And, what do we learn about the proletariat, then and now?

'Revolutionary' Bourgeoisie?

Numerous commentators have noted that whereas the *Manifesto* de-clares the proletariat to be the revolutionary class of the future ('grave-diggers' of the bourgeois order), the great exploits that it narrates are those of the bourgeoisie as it overturns the older order and estab-

---

[6] Aijaz Ahmad, '*The Communist Manifesto* and the Problem of Universality', *Monthly Review*, June 1998.

lishes its dominion over the surface of the entire globe.[7] Some have even made out that Marx suffers from the progressivist ideology of nineteenth century positivism in which the bourgeoisie is the real hero of modernity and history is the history of constant improvement. While the former point has considerable merit, the latter is simply absurd.

The main principle of narration in the *Manifesto* is not that of a teleological unfolding of Progress (a unilinear development that always goes in the direction of greater improvement) but that of a contradictory process of both construction and destruction that proceed simultaneously until the point where the process becomes incapable of resolving or even containing the contradictions it has produced: *that* is the moment of revolutionary rupture, if the proletariat succeeds in making a revolution, or a moment of 'mutual destruction of contending classes', as the *Manifesto* puts it, if no revolutionary resolution is found.[8] If history was always moving in the direction of progress, there would be no need for revolution as such. We shall come momentarily to how Marx, and then later Marxists have conceived of the progressive role of the bourgeoisie in relation to the antecedent modes of production and their correlative political structures. Suffice it to say here that the authors who associated the capitalist mode of production with what the *Manifesto* calls 'a universal

---

[7] The most stimulating statement of this problem can be found in Ellen Meiksins Wood, '*The Communist Manifesto* After 150 Years', in *Monthly Review*, May 1998; reprinted in the new edition of the *Manifesto* issued from the Monthly Review Press, 1998. In the following couple of paragraphs I have drawn upon but also partly departed from that very fine-grained analysis.

[8] Rosa Luxemburg was to summarize these *alternative* possibilities in a pithy phrase when she said that capitalism does not *necessarily* lead to socialism, so that the choice facing humankind was 'socialism *or* barbarism'. Looked at from the vantage-point of today, Marx's own phrase 'mutual destruction of contending classes' is more apt than might appear to those who are unduly impressed by the achieving side of capitalist domination today. Examples are myriad, but we shall confine ourselves to only one. A fundamental contradiction that is inherent in the profit-driven capitalist mode is the destruction – first rather slow, and then increasingly more massive destruction – of a kind of environment that is necessary for sustaining human life, so that we now have an ecologically unsafe planet to the extent that survival of the human species into the coming some centuries cannot be confidently predicted, affecting all the 'contending classes' equally.

war of devastation' or who wrote the following lines, could hardly be thinking of the role of bourgeoisie as simply and mainly a revolutionary role in the positive sense of that word:

> It [capitalism] has resolved personal worth into exchange value, and in place of the numberless, indefeasible chartered freedoms, has set up the single, unconscionable freedom – Free Trade. In one word, for exploitation, veiled by religious and political illusions, it has substituted naked, shameless, direct, brutal exploitation. . . . It has converted the physician, the lawyer, the priest, the poet, the man of science, into its own paid wage-labourers. . . . It compels all bourgeois nations, on pain of extinction, to adopt the bourgeois mode of production; it compels them to introduce what it calls civilization in their midst, i.e., to become bourgeois themselves. In one word, it creates a world in its own image.

That ironic phrase, 'what it calls civilization', reminds one of a superbly contemptuous phrase that Engels was to use later for the colonizing European bourgeoisie: 'civilization-mongers'. This is the language of outrage and denunciation, not of unalloyed enthusiasm.

The other point – that the *Manifesto* treats the proletariat as only an ascendant revolutionary class and tells mainly of the exploits of the bourgeoisie – is certainly correct. This has to do with Marx's punctual method of describing the existing conditions and deducing from them the future directions. It is worth recalling here that even limited trade union rights in the most advanced capitalist country, Britain, were at the time less than a quarter century old; that the first political party which could be viewed as a working class party, namely that of the Chartists, was itself less than a decade old and could hardly be described as 'revolutionary'; even the successful struggle for an 8-hour day was to come very much in the future, and mass working class parties in Europe itself were not to arise until the 1880s, some forty years after the publication of the *Manifesto*. The Communist League, whose manifesto Marx was writing, was a small organization of German emigres in London with even smaller branches in some cities of the Continent. The revolutionary role of the proletariat that Marx was visualizing and theorizing for the future was so very much greater than anything that could be associated with that Communist League that even the name of the organization does not appear in the text of what was its own manifesto. The *Manifesto* does not tell of the revolutionary achievement of the working class for the good reason that in all the revolutions up to that time the proletariat had played a large but a subaltern role, under the flag of the bourgeoisie, and Marx was drafting a call to arms that would put an end to that subaltern position and would for the first time bring the proletariat on to the stage of history as a revolutionary class in its own right. What is important here is not that Marx has no revolutionary exploits of the proletariat to celebrate. What is much more important is the quality of the prediction. If his description of capitalism itself gives us an image of a capitalism not the way it was in 1848 but what it was to become much later, his conception of the revolutionary agent also has that same extraordinary orientation toward the future.

As for the bourgeoisie, it is conceived as a class that has undoubtedly played a revolutionary role in relation to the older regimes of exploitation but, in the same sweep, it is also conceived as class that can no longer extricate itself from the cycle of crises (e.g., 'the epidemic of overproduction') and a 'universal war of devastation'. What, then, has been the revolutionary role?

The *Manifesto* conceives of the bourgeoisie as a *revolutionary* class in two radically different senses, drawing alternately on the very different historical experiences of Britain and France. There is, on the one hand, the *objectively revolutionary* role that has to do mainly with the economic sphere and the social relations necessary for the expanded reproduction of this sphere. Here, Marx draws mainly on the experience of the British capitalist class and focuses on this bourgeoisie's need to constantly revolutionize the forces and relations of production, optimize the pool of the propertyless, maximize the rate of surplus value, generalize the wage relation and 'the cash nexus', and carry market relations to the farthest corner of the earth. This is the logic of industrial capitalism *per se*, and even though only in Britain had such an industrial bourgeoisie fully emerged as the dominant class, Marx had the acumen to see that such was going to be the fate of every other national bourgeoisie which hoped to compete with the more advanced one. Britain was of course to remain in the lead during the rest of his lifetime but other such centres were to soon develop, notably in Germany and the United States even more than France, giving rise to a kind of imperialist rivalry that was qualitatively different from colonial competitions of the mercantilist era.

On the other hand, however, there was also what one might call the *subjectively* revolutionary role of the bourgeoisie which had to do largely with the political sphere and which had been most marked in the French Revolution and the subsequent revolutionary upheavals in many parts of the Continent, including later upheavals within France itself, right up to 1848. Whereas the modern British state had evolved on the basis of a class compromise between the new bourgeoisie and the old aristocracy, with the latter also transforming itself into a bourgeoisie of the ground-rent, as Engels in particular was to emphasize in his writings on Britain, it was the French Revolution, with its Jacobin and even communistic elements, that had sought to fully destroy the *ancien regime* as well as the whole social edifice upon which it had rested. The Restoration there had only led to successive revolutionary upheavals, with the aim of erecting a modern, secular, representative state. If the revolutionary role of the British capitalist class in the economic sphere had led to polarization of classes and universalization of 'the cash nexus', the political revolutions of the French bourgeoisie had sought to create civic and juridic equality of citizens, the class cleavages notwithstanding. If the British bourgeoisie had done all it could to keep the proletariat out of the political process, not even granting a minimum of trade union rights until the third decade of the nineteenth century, the French bourgeoisie had, in each of its revolutionary surges, sought to organize the unprivileged and the proletarianized masses for active participation in the struggle for civic equality, though it too stringently suppressed aspirations of the working classes to organize themselves in autonomous 'combinations' (as these were called at the time). If British political economy had perfected the theory of the free market, the philosophical representatives of the French bourgeoisie had formulated the most extensive thought on social, political, and religious freedoms. And, if British factory production was to set the pattern for later industrializations in the rest of the world, especially in the imperialist core, it was the French theories of 'Liberty, Equality, Fraternity' which have marked the nature of oppositional political agitations right down to our own day. It is in this specific sense that Marxism appropriates the Enlightenment project but also tries to supersede it by concentrating on removing the class virus, and it is precisely on the issue of the class character of the Republican notion of 'freedom' that Marx had criticized the French revolutionary thought the most stringently.

As German settlers in Britain, with intimate knowledge of such places as Paris and Brussels, Marx and Engels well understood this whole range of bourgeois experience in Europe. Nor did they romanticize the 'revolutionary' role of either the British or the French bourgeoisie. If the chapters on primitive accumulation in *Capital* tell the story of the many swindles out of which the British bourgeoisie was born, and if Engels' *Conditions of the Working Class in England* details the moral and material degradation of the great majority that was inherent in the 'revolutionary' phase of the British capitalist class, Marx's mature work was conceived as a *critique* of primarily British political economy as an illusory science that merely reflects the phenomenal form of the capitalist mode of production; *inter alia*, he shows how unfree the so-called 'free market' really is, and how freedom of the market itself leads to monopoly. Similarly, in analyses of the British state, they had shown how much the aristocracy had been absorbed in its key institutions, especially the Armed Forces and the colonial governments. As for the French Revolution, Marx had contemptuously written of 'the self-conceit of the political sphere' precisely in relation to the French representative state and its juridic equalities, and as early as 'The Jewish Question' (1843), well before the *Manifesto*, he had also shown, through careful analyses of the 'Declaration of the Rights of Man' and of key clauses of the French Constitution, how juridic equality was based on much more fundamental inequalities and how the right to private property is the most fundamental right guaranteed therein. In their numerous writings, Marx and Engels make quite explicit the distinction between the British and French experiences, showing how neither is capable of completing the revolutions they have set in motion; as the *Manifesto* puts it, 'The conditions of bourgeois society are too narrow to encompass the wealth created by them'.

In the condensed, epic prose of the *Manifesto*, however, they present these two tales of the respective bourgeoisies as a single story of the structural imperative inherent in the generalization of the capitalist mode of production as such, as if the bourgeoisie that had revolutionized the forces of production was the same that was revolutionizing the political structures. Some writers, including many admirers of this text, have viewed this condensing of the respective experiences into one as a weakness, an over-generalization and an inaccurate characterization of the French bourgeoisie. That is to a certain extent true. The weakness would surely be more significant if we were dealing with a descriptive text that would require distinctions of that kind. In stead, the very method of the *Manifesto* assumes that each national bourgeoisie shall grow in historical conditions specific to it and that in the process of its own maturation each national bourgeoisie is beset with its own set of anachronisms and its own realities of uneven development. What is of central importance, however, is that no mature system of capitalist production can arise without generalized 'free' labour which must then be translated, sooner or later, into juridic equality, all the more so because this formal equality of otherwise unequal citizens is itself a reflection of the capitalist market that organizes commodity exchange in the language of equivalences. Thus, it did not matter, from the historical standpoint of the long-term trend, that production in the Southern United States of Marx's own time was based on unfree, slave labour, despite the Bill of Rights that had bravely, and with no small degree of duplicity, proclaimed that 'All men are created equal'. What mattered, rather, was that the United States could not emerge as a uniform labour market and an industrialized society without, sooner or later, abolishing slavery and establishing some kind of juridic equality among its citizens. That process spanned over a hundred years or so, from the abolition of slavery during the 1860s to the Civil Rights legislations and movements of the 1950s and 1960s. But the process did occur, even though that newly-won juridic equality rests on top of a whole heap of social and economic inequalities, along lines of race as well as class.

But this question of the revolutionary role of the bourgeoisie we could approach from another angle as well. Since the *Manifesto*, many Marxists have addressed a particular question: when does the bourgeoisie *cease* to be a revolutionary class? At the most general level, Lenin argued that the decisive turn in Europe came with (a) the completion of the process of forming nation-states in the latter half of the nineteenth century; (b) the emergence of the revolutionary movements of the working class during roughly the same time; and (c) the onset of imperialism which established the supremacy of 'coupon-clippers' within Europe and prevented the consolidation of the classes of modern capitalism in the colonies – an onset that Lenin dates also from about the 1880s. Within the colonies, however, the emergent national bourgeoisies could play a constructive role in anti-colonial struggles but the attempt had to be made to organize a leading role for worker–peasant coalitions within the liberation struggles. For Russia itself, Lenin argued that capitalism had produced sufficient concentrations of the proletariat in key areas of class conflict for the struggle for a socialist revolution to begin, and that contradictions of Russian capitalism were such that neither the economic task of further, full-fledged, independent industrialization nor the political task of creating a modern state could be left to the bourgeoisie.

Generally, Marxists have tended to argue that the shift in the role of the bourgeoisie as a 'revolutionary' class comes between the aborted revolutions of 1848, immediately after the publication of the *Manifesto*, and the short-lived Paris Commune of 1871. In other words, the bourgeoisie's fear of the proletarianized masses which was already palpable during the revolutions of 1848 turned, after the Commune, into a full-fledged nightmare of a possible proletarian revolution. Antonio Gramsci, however, makes an arresting point. He argues that the bourgeoisie's fear of the proletariat goes back to the French Revolution itself. It had fully mobilized the proletarianized masses in the course of its own struggle against the *ancien regime*, but then counterrevolutionary terror came as soon as it became clear that the masses were gathering on a platform of radical equality, with increasing talk of the abolition of property and full democratization of state administration, that threatened the supremacy of the bourgeoisie itself. The masses were of course suppressed. Gramsci argues that the European bourgeoisie learned from that experience so well that in every subsequent revolutionary upheaval the bourgeoisie always compromised with the landowning classes in defence of the rule of property as such.

He traces the reactionary character of the bourgeois regimes in nineteenth century Europe, especially in Germany and Italy, to this enduring class compromise on the part of the bourgeoisie. In the case of Italy, with which he was mainly concerned, he argues that the weakness of parliamentary democracy and the rise of fascism were both related to the crisis created by the rise of the most modern capitalist relations arising in one sector of the economy, mostly in Northern Italy, and the most backward and anachronistic structures persisting in the rest of the country, especially in the South. This extreme form of uneven development he traces to the fact that the bourgeoisie never really confronted the landowning classes, even though it played a relatively progressive role in obtaining independence and unity of the Italian nation-state. According to this argument, then, the revolutionary role of the bourgeoisie came and went rather quickly.

This sheds interesting light on the role of the bourgeoisie in India. Some sections of it certainly played a progressive role during the struggle for Independence. However, five countervailing factors should also be noted. First, key sectors of the Indian bourgeoisie, such as the house of Tata, remained closer to the colonial authority than to the national movement. Second, even those who drew closer to the national movement, mainly through Gandhi's mediation, such as the Birlas, adopted an attitude of collaborative competition with regard to the colonial authority, while fully anti-colonial positions were more common among sections of the smaller bourgeoisie. Third, the bourgeoisie was always suspicious of mass movements and, during the crucial two years between the end of the Second World War and the moment of Independence, as the revolutionary wave began to rise, the bourgeois leadership was no less keen on a quick settlement than the British themselves, even if it meant partition of the country; better partition than revolution, it effectively said. Fourth, after Independence the bourgeoisie made a far-reaching alliance with the landed classes, old and new, making impossible land reforms that would radically alter the conditions of life for the poor peasants, the rural proletariat, the bonded labourers, the *adivasis* and the like. It thus pre-empted the chance of extensive social reforms in the antiquated, traditional society which are simply not possible without radical re-distribution of land and other agricultural resources in the first place.

The most advanced forms of capitalist development in some areas has been combined with the most extensive backwardness of social and property relations in much of the country. Much of the social pathology we witness today, giving rise to all manner of fascistoid violences, is ultimately rooted in this fact. Finally, the fear of the proletariat and the peasantry has meant that this bourgeoisie has found it easier to compromise with imperialism than to undertake radical transformation of Indian society, even for its own purposes; they would rather have an extremely restricted home market and an unhealthy, socially backward, illiterate or semi-literate work-force than undertake a social transformation that may slip out of their control. In stead of a 'revolutionary' bourgeoisie, we have something of a permanent, pre-emptive counterrevolution, which only goes to show that in a society such as the one we have, even the tasks of a bourgeois revolution cannot be fully carried out except within a socialist transition.

Are There 'Laws' of Capitalism?

Schematically speaking, we could say that the *Manifesto*, and the science of Marxism of which this is a document of very great importance, is built around two kinds of principles or 'laws'. One set consists of 'laws' pertaining to the very motion of the capitalist mode of production which are fundamental and immutable throughout the whole history of this mode, without which capitalism would cease to be capitalism as such. Three such laws can be summarized here, simply to illustrate a part of this theoretical core, or what Marx might have called the 'rational kernel' of this theory.

There is, first, the proposition that throughout its history, capitalism drives toward greater and greater polarization between the fundamental classes. This does not mean that no intermediate classes or strata are present at any given time; indeed, with the increasing complexity of administration, management and technical expertise required for expanded reproduction of capital, such intermediate strata arise all along the axis of this class polarization. What the law means, rather, is that the means of production for the expanded reproduction of capital tend to get concentrated at one end of the class polar-

ization, while the increasingly more numerous majority gets proletarianized (i.e., loses control over these means of production) and is
forced to sell its labour-power, whether in the 'organized' or the 'unorganized' sector, and whether on the full-time, permanent basis or
as casual and temporary labourers. 'Repression' or 'poverty' are punctual features of this class relation, but what defines it as specifically
'capitalist' is the category of 'exploitation', i.e., expanded reproduction and accumulation of capital by one class that appropriates the
labour-power of the other class. It is in relation to this polarization of
classes that the concept of class struggle is derived, and the main point
is that all classes, especially the two polar classes, the bourgeoisie and
the proletariat, participate in this struggle. We tend to think of class
struggle only in relation to the proletariat, as revolutionary struggle.
Marx's point is that the possessing class itself wages a brutal and permanent struggle in defence of its own class interests, through violence and threats of violence, through exploitations both extensive
and intensive, by maintaining a permanent army of the unemployed,
and through thousand other means in the social, political, economic,
ideological and cultural arenas. Class struggle has, in other words,
not one side but two.

Second, there is the iron 'law' of increasing globalization of the
capitalist mode of production, first extensively by bringing more and
more territories and populations under its dominion, and then in-
tensively by constantly imposing newer and newer labour regimes
and processes of production, which are first invented at the core of
the system and then get enforced in its peripheries as and when the
need arises. This globalizing tendency was there well before the Industrial Revolution came about and is an ongoing process today, in
myriad forms. No pre-capitalist mode had this constant expansion as
an inherent law of its own reproduction; capitalism does. The feudal
lords of Britain had neither the design nor the capacity to extend their
feudal mode into the rest of the world; the British bourgeoisie was
increasingly embroiled in perfecting precisely such designs and ca-
pacities. Today, when some celebrated theorists in the advanced capitalist countries are talking of 'late capitalism', 'post-imperialist capitalism', even a 'postmodern' and 'cybernetic' capitalism in which production is said to have been replaced by information technologies,

the basic fact is that, according to the calculations of the World Bank, the number of workers in the 'modern' (i.e. fully capitalist) sector has doubled during the thirty years between 1965 and 1995, the very years when capitalism is said to have abolished historic forms of labour (a book was recently published in the United States, by eminent labour theorists in the postmodern Left, simply called *Post-Work*).

The third such law that we can cite as a permanent feature of capitalism is the class nature of the state, i.e., that no capitalist society can exist and reproduce itself without a state that is the state of the bourgeoisie as a whole. Now, on the Left at least, we take this for granted. On Marx's part, this was a revolutionary discovery. For the political theory that he had inherited, from the Enlightenment and the French Revolution and right up to Hegel, the normal and desirable state was one that stood above all classes and fractions of civil society, mediating their disputes and itself embodying the General Will. It is in this sense that Hegel had described the bureaucracy as 'a universal class'; in other words, a class that represented not the interest of a particular class but a universal interest, of the whole society. It is directly in response to Hegel's description of the bureaucracy as the universal class that Marx was to say so emphatically that only the proletariat is *potentially* a universal class, since as an object of universal exploitation it has no particular interests to defend, and that the proletariat can actually *become* such a 'universal class' through a revolutionary re-structuring of society into one where 'the free development of each is the precondition for the free development of all' – free, above all, from exploitation. This definition of 'freedom' – as a freedom, first of all, from exploitation – was also a new one. Through a dense and brilliant analysis of some founding texts of the French Revolution – 'Declaration of the Rights of Man' as well as some key clauses of the Republican Constitution – Marx had shown in 'The Jewish Question' that the fundamental freedom granted by the Declaration is the right to private property, that the fundamental right granted was the right to defend one's property against encroachment by others, and that the core of legal government were laws pertaining to right and freedom of property. This, he argued, was certainly an advance over the arbitrary powers of the monarchical state, but, in a dialectical move, freedom from exploitation was now posited as the *true* freedom that could only be guaranteed through abolition of capitalism as such, as against the *illusory* and class-based freedom of private property as guaranteed by documents of the bourgeois revolution. The main point, in any case, was that a state that guaranteed the right to private property, hence the system of exploitation, could not possibly represent, either in theory or in practice, the General Will. Such a state had to be a class state, and that class society could not be abolished without simultaneously abolishing the class state.

Such are some of the fundamental 'laws' of motion under capitalism, and without some strict conception of such laws Marxism ceases to be a coherent theory. This does not mean that such laws function in exactly the same way in all places and all times. It does mean, though, that capitalism cannot exist without the operation of such laws. However, most of what passes for 'laws of history' or 'laws of nature' and even 'laws of political economy' are in fact what we might call *laws of tendency*, i.e., the view that since capitalism is on the whole an intelligible structure a correct understanding of the existing structure can reasonably predict that, all else being equal, certain phenomena would tend to take particular directions and particular forms. For example, Marx speaks in the *Manifesto* of the inherent tendency of capitalism toward periodic crises, and he speaks specifically of 'the epidemic of overproduction'. In later, more mature studies of political economy, he was to closely demonstrate that the inherent tendency in the average rate of capitalist profit was toward decline, thanks to competitions of various sorts, crises of overproduction, etc. These are obviously laws of tendency that gives to capitalism a peculiarly unstable character. However, the rate of profit does not *always* fall, not in every period, not in every branch of production, not in all phases of the class struggle, not in every national space of investment. The bourgeoisie is always trying to maintain at least a constant, if not rising, rate of profit. Much of the drive behind imperialist expansion and exploitation of more and more regions and peoples of the world is precisely to stabilize and push up these rates in the core countries; and the bourgeoisie wages an unremitting class struggle against workers everywhere to simultaneously raise the productivity of labour, depress the wage rate and yet expand the market for its products – by raising, for example, the level of consumer debt, by extending to them a purchasing power beyond their earned incomes, so that the capitalists can sell their products while also collecting interest on the generalized debt. We have, in other words, not a teleological unfolding of an iron law but the contradictory structure of tendencies and counter-tendencies.

Broadly speaking, the guiding principle here is that, as Engels was to put it, 'men make their own history but they make it in circumstances given to them'. History is, in other words, a dynamic and ever changing mix of intentions and constraints. The choices people make and the outcomes they produce are deeply constrained by the 'circumstances given to them'. However, they could not make 'their own history' if intentions did not matter and if tendencies inherent in the system could not be reversed. Indeed, revolution is a moment where intentions – the subjective factor; the collective human agency – would confront the constraints and transform them in radically new directions.

Globalization, Economy, and Culture

This distinction between laws that are fundamental to the structure as a whole and laws that are only laws of tendency can be grasped if we look at the way the *Manifesto* speaks of (a) the process of globalization strictly in terms of the expansion of capital on the one hand, and (b) on the other, the probable consequences it attempts to foresee in diverse other areas, such as on the issue of 'national specificity' or on the issue of a 'world literature' arising in the distant future out of the dissolution of national literatures.

It is really quite extraordinary how frequently words like 'global' and 'universal' appear in the brief first part of the *Manifesto*. A very considerable conquest of the globe had been happening since at least the early part of the sixteenth century, driven largely by very powerful merchants' capital. The colonization of the Americas, the extermination of the bulk of their populations, the mass enslavement of Africans (thirty million slaves shipped out of Africa, with half of them dying before reaching the American and Caribbean shores), the network of trading and military posts all along the coasts of Africa and Asia, the virtually complete colonization of India itself – all this, and much more, had happened by the time the *Manifesto* was drafted. Indeed, the process had been much accelerated after the Industrial Revolution (it was actually Engels who was to call it that). Between 1770 and 1848, the British alone acquired Australia, New Zealand, South Africa, in addition to most of India, while France took chunks of North Africa.

How different was Marx's view of all that can be gauged from the fact that Hegel, the philosopher whom Marx admired as well as fought against the most, had seen in this wave of colonization a necessary and welcome solution, one almost ordained by nature itself, for the surplus population of Europe. Marx's great achievement was that he saw this process as part of what the *Manifesto* calls a 'universal war of devastation', connected it all with the inherent nature of capitalism, and then tried to make this perception a key element in the consciousness of the European working class itself. It needs to be said, however, that the colonialism of his day was nothing like the imperialism about which Lenin was to write some seventy years later and the beginning of which Lenin himself was to date around the 1880s, i.e., not in the days of Marx's youth but in the very last years of his life. And, during the seventy years since Lenin wrote his famous pamphlet, *Imperialism, the Highest Stage of Capitalism*, some of the basic features of imperialism have again changed more radically than they did during the previous seventy years.

The astonishing fact is that when Marx writes specifically of the economic and technological expansion of capitalism on a global scale, and of the deep penetration of capitalist logic into regions very remote from Europe, today's reader tends to think not of the capitalism and colonialism of Marx's time but the capitalism and imperialism of our own time – despite all the historic shifts that have taken place and that have transformed the processes of globalization in very fundamental ways. He asserts that 'modern industry has established the world market', that 'the bourgeoisie . . . must nestle everywhere, settle everywhere, establish connections everywhere', and that 'in place of the old local and national seclusion and self-sufficiency, we have intercourse in every direction, universal inter-dependence of nations everywhere' – at a time when most of Europe itself, let alone the rest of the world, did not have industrial economies. Even France was then an overwhelmingly rural society and Germany, which was to emerge by the end of the nineteenth century as one of three most industrialized societies alongside Britain and France, was at that time not even a unified nation-state. Similarly, Marx speaks here of capitalism's drive to unify the globe through a 'revolution' in transport – at a time when steamboats and railways were a bare novelty. The first steamboat had sailed from the Americas to Europe in 1819, and as late as 1840 railways in England itself covered merely 843 miles of track. Yet the vivid metaphors of speed and compression that Marx employs in speaking of the world having been transformed into a single entity through industry, technology, the global chase of commodities and the 'cash nexus', conjures up in the reader's mind today's world of jet travel, international TV channels, globalized patterns of fashions and fast foods, and the computerized network of stock exchanges across the globe where billions of dollars can be moved around in seconds. In rapid, sharp strokes necessary for so brief a text, Marx condenses description and prediction in a single sweep. He sees what is there already, and he grasps the long-range dynamics at work behind and beyond what he actually sees, so that if one sentence of the *Manifesto* gives us the capitalism of 1848 the very next one gives us an image of what was yet to be, in the indefinite future, right up to our own and beyond. What is of key importance here is the firmness and accuracy with which Marx was able to perceive the future development of capitalism by grasping its inexorable operative laws.

But there is also a structure of secondary formulations – also regarding 'globalization' – essentially deductive and speculative in nature, about the likely consequences of this capitalist logic as it was expected to unfold in diverse areas of national formations, the arts, etc. Several of those formulations had to do with the kind of world European expansion into the rest of the world was to make. Here, in areas that are at some distance from economy as such, and which are areas essentially of political and cultural forms, two kinds of problems arise. The first, and in the long run less significant historically and theoretically, is the uncritical use of some inherited categories which was at best unpleasant, e.g., the description of capitalist Europe and precapitalist China as 'civilized and 'barbarian' respectively. The second kind of problem pertains to the kind of expectation which subsequent history has proved to be wrong, especially in relation to the colonized countries. As colonialism fully matured and at length gave us what Lenin was to designate as 'imperialism', which is still very much with us, national differences, far from disappearing, in fact became more recalcitrant and more hierarchically structured. Nationalism itself was to have a history very different from what we can deduce from the *Manifesto*. Some of the correctives came in the later writings of Marx and Engels themselves, other and even more substantive ones came from a later generation of Marxists, Lenin and Rosa Luxemburg in particular.

When Marx drafted the *Manifesto* he had studied great many things, but there is very little evidence that he had really studied the whole complexity of the colonial enterprise. It was only later, after the revolutions of 1848 had been defeated and he settled down to a life-long exile in London the next year, that he undertook any systematic study of colonialism, especially after Engels persuaded him to undertake the writing of some journalistic pieces for the *New York Herald Tribune* regularly, mainly in order to make a little money. This study then meant that both Marx and Engels started paying much greater attention to the actual events of colonial history as it unfolded over the next three or four decades, and this they did to the extent that it was possible to grasp those events from accounts in the British press. As I have argued at some length elsewhere, it was in those later years that Marx became much more thoroughly disillusioned with the 'progressive' results that he had expected of colonialism earlier, in his youth, and that both he and Engels began affirming the right of resistance on the part of the colonized peoples.[9]

---

[9] Aijaz Ahmad, *In Theory: Classes, Nations, Literatures*, London 1992; Delhi 1994; pp. 228–29. Two passages, from Marx and Engels respectively, should clarify this point. The first, from Marx, occurs in a letter written rather late in life (to Danielson, in 1881):

> In India serious complications, if not a general outbreak, are in store for the British government. What the British take from them annually in the form of rent, dividends for railways useless for the Hindoos, pensions for the military and civil servicemen, for Afghanistan and other wars, etc.,

With all the benefits of hindsight one hundred and fifty years later, one can make four points with some degree of certainty. One is that Marx and Engels themselves were to understand the phenomenon of colonialism much better in later years than they did at the time of writing the *Manifesto*; in 1847–48, they fully understood the key role of colonialism in the global expansion of the capitalist mode but not that, far from unifying the globe politically, colonialism would divide and sub-divide the world into numerous entities large and small, so that 'national specificity' would on the whole rather increase than decline.[10] Second, even though they understood colonialism much better in later years, the structure itself was to alter very drastically and a wholly more complex and in some ways quite different theoretical apparatus would then be required, which was to be the focus of attention for a later generation of Marxists, Lenin most particularly, but also Bukharin, Luxemburg, Hilferding, and some of the

> etc., – what they take from them *without any equivalent* and *quite apart* from what they appropriate to themselves annually *within* India, – speaking only of *the value of the commodities* that Indians have to gratuitously and annually *send over* to England – it amounts to *more than the total sum of the income of the 60 million of agricultural and industrial laborers of India.* This is a bleeding process with a vengeance. [Italics in the original]

And, well before Marx referred to colonialism as a 'bleeding process with a vengeance', Engels had this to say about what we today call 'national liberation':

> There is evidently a different spirit among the Chinese now. . . . The mass of people take an active, nay, a fanatical part in the struggle against the foreigners. They poison the bread of the European community at Hongkong by wholesale, and with the coolest meditation. . . . The very coolies emigrating to foreign countries rise in mutiny, and as if by concert, on board every emigrant ship, fight for its possession. . . . Civilization mongers who throw hot shell on a defenseless city and add rape to murder, may call the system cowardly, barbarous, atrocious; but what matter it to the Chinese if it be but successful? . . . We had better recognize that this is a war *pro aris et focis*, a popular war for the maintenance of Chinese nationality. ('Persia and China', 1857)

10 In the imperialist core this 'national specificity' is of course declining at the current, far more mature stage, as indicated for example in the ongoing European integration. Such was not to be the case in the rest of the globe, however, and even in Europe this is a very recent and still very, very uneven process.

Austro–Marxists such as Otto Bauer, who were to make very seminal contribution to theories of colonialism as well as nationalism. Third, if the political consequences could not be gauged with precision, less still was it possible to do so with respect to the cultural consequences; far from there arising a 'world literature' in any meaningful sense, as the *Manifesto* had envisioned, the cultural consequences of colonialism were such that the literatures of the colonized people were to remain regional and/or national, while in the global marketplace of capitalism they were always subordinated to the literatures of the advanced metropoles. Finally, Marx's own discovery that the rate and quantum of change under capitalism is greater than under any previous mode, and that this rate of change increases in every succeeding phase, also means that the world has by now changed so very much since the time not only of Marx but also of Lenin or even Gramsci that an immense new theoretical labour is required to understand the world as we now have it.

This discrepancy between the stunning prescience of Marx's summation of the fundamental structure in the strictly economic sphere, and the much less assured a touch in foreseeing the coming changes in some of the political and cultural spheres, can perhaps be looked at from another angle as well. Several years after drafting the *Manifesto*, in a famous formulation in his 'Preface' to *A Critique of Political Economy* of 1859, Marx was to write:

> . . . a distinction should always be made between the material transformation of the economic conditions of production, which can be determined with the precision of natural science, and the legal, political, religious, aesthetic, or philosophic – in short, ideological forms in which men become conscious of their conflict and fight it out.

What is striking about this distinction is that only 'the transformation of the economic conditions of production' are said to be available for being 'determined with precision', in a scientific manner. The 'consciousness' of that fundamental conflict is said to belong elsewhere – in 'the legal, political, religious, aesthetic, or philosophic' forms – which evidently cannot be 'determined' with equal 'precision' even though – or, more likely, *because* – that is where people actually 'fight it out', so that, presumably, those forms are less the outcome of objective structural laws and much more 'determined' by the very way human subjects 'fight it out' in collective struggles that take not only 'legal, political' forms but also 'religious, aesthetic, or philosophic' forms. According to this principle, then, it is only logical that Marx could foresee with far greater precision much of the course that the globalization of the capitalist mode of *economic* production was to take but could not predict with anything like that degree of precision what 'political' or 'aesthetic' forms were to ensue.

Proletariat, the 'Universal Class'

Marx conceptualized the proletariat as a 'universal class' at a time when no country in Asia or Africa could be considered as having something resembling a modern proletariat. In the larger American countries, like the U.S. and Brazil, there were many more slaves than proletarians. Russia was steeped in serfdom; certainly the whole of Eastern and Southern Europe, and much of the rest as well, was predominantly agrarian. The term 'universal class' was used, I believe, in two senses. The first was in part a philosophical proposition: since what all proletarians have in common is an experience of exploitation and a location in processes of production that were collective as well as impersonal, they had an inherent (within the class, a universal) interest in a revolution against the system of exploitation as such; and since the system of exploitation could not be abolished piecemeal, nor could it be abolished without abolishing *both* capital and 'wage-slavery' at the same time, along with all the political, social and ideological superstructures that arose on the premise of that exploitation, the proletariat could not emancipate itself without abolishing the system as a whole, emancipating society as a whole; it was the class *par excellance* of universal emancipation.

That was the first sense and, as pointed out earlier, it was initially a philosophical proposition posited in opposition to Hegel's description of the *bureaucracy* as a 'universal class'. But there was also the other sense that since capital had an inherent drive toward globalization, i.e., toward establishing its dominion in all corners of the earth, it was destined to constantly increase the number of proletarians around the globe so that, eventually, the proletariat would come to be comprised of the great majority of humanity, spread universally in all parts of the world: a world proletariat, in other words, over and above all national bounds. Universal in *scale* as well! This was also projected as a process of greater class polarization ('simplification of the class structure', as the *Manifesto* calls it) as well as absolute immiseration of the majority.

This is what has now come to pass, for the first time in history: not in Marx's time, not in Lenin's time, but in ours.

I have mentioned earlier that according to World Bank calculations the number of proletarians doubled in the course of the thirty years between 1965 and 1995. This number is now said to stand at roughly two and a half billion (i.e., two thousand five hundred million) of whom 120 million are said to be currently unemployed, roughly one billion are said to subsist on less than a dollar a day, and many unknown millions are said to have stopped looking for work. Needless to add that the overwhelming majority of this immiserated bulk lives in the poorer continents of Asia, Africa, and Latin america. For China alone, the World Bank calculates that there is, besides the employed and semi-employed proletariat, already a 'floating population' of 80 million who have ceased to be peasants and are not yet part of the 'modern' sector and that over a hundred more million peasants will leave the Chinese countryside over the next decade or so to look for work in the cities. Similar processes are at work in other countries of Asia, Africa and Latin America as well. The same statistics also suggest that no more than 12 to 15 per cent of labouring activity is now left on the surface of this earth which is not in one way or another, directly or remotely, connected with the world market; well over 80 per cent now produces for this integrated market – a novel 'universalization' in its own terms. As regards increasing immiseration, the May 1998 issue of *Monthly Review* published the following statistical table about shifts of wealth from the poor and the middling to the rich over a short span between 1965 and 1990:

SHARES OF WORLD INCOME, PER CENT

	1965	1990
Poorest 20 per cent	2.3	1.4
Second 20 per cent	2.9	1.8
Third 20 per cent	4.2	2.1
Fourth 20 per cent	21.2	11.3
Richest 20 per cent	69.5	83.4

The long and short of it is that for 80 per cent of the people around the globe share of wealth was cut by half in the course of barely 25 years, or over roughly a single generation, while the share of the lower 40 per cent at the later point dropped to just over 3 per cent of the total. What is also significant is that the share of the second highest 20 per cent – presumably, the so-called 'middle class' or even perhaps 'upper middle class' – also saw its share in total wealth cut by almost half. So much for the expansion or the financial security of this 'middle class'! For the average share to be cut so drastically, at least a good number must have fallen into the category of 'low income' or even 'poor' and great many more must have seen their standards of living decline sharply and perhaps their levels of indebtedness rising pro-portionately. What is striking in any case is the absolute polarization: roughly 3 per cent of the income for 40 per cent of the people and 83 per cent of the wealth for the top 20 per cent.

Thus, increasing polarization, immiseration, proletarianization and primitive accumulation are ongoing processes in our own time. In the imperialist centres of the world which have experienced the highest concentration of accumulated capital, and where the processes of proletarianization and primitive accumulation were completed earlier, the emphasis has shifted more toward intensive exploitation and accumulation of relative surplus value, based on more advanced technologies. In formations of backward capital, the intensity of labour rather than of capital is still very substantially at the heart of 'global-ization'; for China, which has had spectacular though now declining success in expanding its exports, something like three-fourths of all exports are now labour-intensive whereas less than forty per cent were labour-intensive a decade ago when the volume of exports was much more limited. The great increase in exports is owed, in other words, not so much to any technological 'modernization' of the process of production but to the more methodical, more intensified exploitation of labour.

Simply in terms of the global spread, the proletariat is now infinitely more 'universal' than ever before, which then means that, in objective terms, the imperative for workers of the world to unite is greater than ever before. This universal proletarianization does not come without its own problems, however. As David Harvey puts it:

> The workforce is now far more geographically dispersed, culturally heterogeneous, ethnically and religiously diverse, racially stratified, and linguistically fragmented. . . . Differentials (both geographical and social) in wages and social provision within the global working class are likewise greater than they have ever been.[11]

Problems of this kind, as regards stratification within the working class, which compound the difficulty of obtaining working class unity, are then further compounded by several other factors such as increasing proportion of casual and temporary work as against more secure full-time employment; increasing weight of the 'unorganized' sector relative to the 'organized' one; great mobility and transience of the labour force, as well as the greater mobility of capital itself, and so on.

In sum, then, capital has more than completed what was once conceived as its historic mission: it has created a single world market and it has taken the process of proletarianization deep into the farthest nook and corner of this earth. Obtaining working class unity, starting at the point of habitation and production and spiralling up to national levels and across the nation-states, shall be the more exacting task for militants of a socialism yet to come. When the *Manifesto* reminds us that 'every class struggle is in essence a political

---

[11] David Harvey, 'The Geography of Class Power', *The Socialist Register 1998*, Merlin Press (in UK) and Monthly Press (in USA), 1998.

struggle' it calls upon us to recognize that same distinction which I tried to clarify a bit earlier with the help of Marx's formulation in his 'Preface' to *A Critique of Political Economy* of 1859. Let me repeat that formulation for greater emphasis:

> . . . a distinction should always be made between the material transformation of the economic conditions of production, which can be determined with the precision of natural science, and the legal, political, religious, aesthetic, or philosophic – in short, ideological forms in which men become conscious of their conflict and fight it out.

In order to transform the class struggle that is forever going on in 'material transformation of the economic conditions of production' into a properly 'political struggle', all the 'ideological forms in which men become conscious of their conflict and fight it out' – legal, political, religious, aesthetic, or philosophic forms – need to be addressed together. Otherwise, those issues of subjective consciousness and objective stratification which divide the working classes of the world cannot be addressed. The more diverse the populations that get proletarianized, the more diverse will have to be the forms that are designed to bring about that unity. For, as the scope of proletarianization has escalated rapidly, every 'political struggle' has become accordingly more complex, encompassing a greater variety of 'forms' ('religious, aesthetic' etc). For, one bitter lesson we have learned in the course of this process is that the fact of immiseration itself does not produce a consciousness of class unity. For that, the domain of consciousness has to be addressed in the very forms in which it experiences the world, and those forms are social and ideological in nature.

Irfan Habib

The Reading of History in *The Communist Manifesto*

Set to draft

The Communist Manifesto for publication early in 1848, Marx and Engels were called upon to give a popular form to their understanding of philosophy, history, economics and politics, and to frame a practical programme on this basis. The effort was at once both summation and creation: summation of principles that they had come to grasp both independently and together in the preceding five years, and creation to deal with lacunae that to be filled up. The task was brilliantly performed making the *Manifesto* undoubtedly the most important single document in the annals of the Communist movement. There is no need of special justification, therefore, to analyse its contents with exceptional care.

The Communist Manifesto is a product of that basic departure from the materialism of the Young Hegelians which led to the initial formulation of Marx's own conception of history. In 1845 when he wrote his Theses on Feuerbach, the very first thesis was as follows:

> The chief defect of all previous materialism – that of Feuerbach included – is that things, reality, sensuousness are conceived only in the form of the *object, or of contemplation*, but not as *sensuous human activity, practice*, not subjectively. . . . Feuerbach wants sensuous objects, really distinct from conceptual objects, but he does not conceive human activity itself as *objective* activity.

The matter is further elaborated in the third thesis:

> The [Feuerbachian] materialist doctrine concerning the changing of circumstances and upbringing forgets that circumstances are changed by men and that the educator must himself be educated.

The theses lead up to the following celebrated finale:

> The philosophers have only *interpreted* the world in various ways; the point is to *change* it.[1]

The crucial importance of these Theses has often been ignored by critics of Marxism (and, unluckily, some of its followers as well), who attribute to it a very determinist aspect, as if 'material' factors simply determine consciousness, which then merely serves as a

---

[1] 'Theses on Feuerbach', the original version, as published in English translation in Karl Marx and Frederick Engels, *Collected Works*, V, Moscow 1976, pp. 3–5. Emphasis as in the original. The final thesis reappears in *The German Ideology*, composed by Marx and Engels in 1845–46, in the following words: '. . . in reality and for the *practical* materialist, i.e. the *communist*, it is a question of revolutionizing the existing world, of practically coming to grips with and changing the things found in existence'. Ibid., pp. 38–39. The portion containing this passage seems to be omitted in S. Ryazanskaya's translation of *The German Ideology*, Moscow 1964; it should have come on p. 39.

medium for bringing about changes that those material circumstances have made 'inevitable'. Such interpretations have often relied upon Marx's Preface to *A Contribution to the Critique of Political Economy* (1859), in which he speaks of how 'the mode of production of material life conditions the general process of social, political and intellectual life,' and goes on to assert that 'it is not the consciousness of men that determines their existence but, on the contrary their social existence that determines their consciousness'.[2]

But if we look at these words closely, we musk ask, what, after all, 'production of material life' consists in. Surely, human labour (and, therefore, human consciousness) is the driving element behind all processes of production, and man's social being itself is the result in a large part of his own practice. The 'consciousness' that man's social being 'determines' or sets limits to is, then, only what stands outside the realm of material production, the seemingly pure realm of intellect. The position is clarified in Marx's conclusion that mankind always 'sets itself only such tasks as it is able to solve; since closer examination will always show that the problem itself arises only when the material conditions for its solution are already present or at least in the course of formation'.[3] It, however, still remains of decisive moment for human intellects to correctly discover the soluble question and define its solution: 'the educator must himself be educated'. And once individuals have grasped the questions to be taken up, the ideas attained have to be propagated in order to have practical consequence. This surely constitutes 'the significance of "revolutionary", of "practical–critical", activity' of which Marx speaks in his Theses on Feuerbach.[4] Gramsci, the Italian Communist thinker in his *Prison Notebooks* argued insightfully that 'fatalism' (i.e. determinism, the belief in the inevitability of a certain process) is at best 'the clothing worn by real and active will when in a weak position'. He urged that 'it is essential to demonstrate the futility of mechanical determinism'; for otherwise it would become 'a cause of passivity, of idiotic

---

[2] *A Contribution to the Critique of Political Economy*, translated by S. Ryazanskaya, edited by M. Dobb, Moscow 1978, pp. 20–21.
[3] Ibid., p. 21.
[4] Marx and Engels, *Collected Works*, V, p. 1.

self-sufficiency' – a fatal position for any revolutionary movement.[5]

While Marx and Engels paid full attention to limits on immediate 'practice', set by the historically inherited circumstances, they did not subscribe to any belief in any automatic or blind force of history. The action to change the world could come only by the diffusion of ideas leading to revolutionary practice. It was, therefore, inherent in the philosophical conclusions they had reached in 1845–46, that they should now come forward with a clear clarion call for revolution – which was the main object of *The Communist Manifesto*. The *Manifesto* is thus a splendid monument to the confident belief of Marxism's founding fathers that it was for thinking men, not blind 'matter', to rise and overthrow the existing order.

II

Complementing Marx's and Engels's belief that theory must lead to revolutionary practice, was their application of the dialectical method to history, which implies that changes are to be seen as the results of the interplay of contradictions. Dialectics came to Marx from Hegel, but, as he put it in his Preface to the second German edition of *Capital*, I (1873), the 'mystified form' which had been given to dialectics by Hegel needed to be transformed into a 'rational form'. In this form,

> it [dialectics] includes in its comprehension and affirmative recognition of the existing state of things, at the same time also the recognition of the negation of that state, of its inevitable breaking up, because it regards every historically developed social form as in fluid movement, and therefore takes into account its transient nature not less than its momentary existence, because it lets nothing impose upon it and is in its essence critical and revolutionary.

---

[5] *Selections from the Prison Notebooks of Antonio Gramsci*, edited and translated by Quintin Hoare and Geoffrey Nowell Smith, New York 1971, pp. 336–37. Also see Louis Althusser, *For Marx*, translated by Ben Brewster, Harmondsworth 1969, pp. 105–06, n. 23.

And he then goes on to speak of the 'contradictions inherent in the movement of capitalist society'.[6]

Whether what Marx did with Hegel's dialectics was merely an inversion ('turned right side up again', as Marx said in the Preface above quoted), or a fundamental 'break' with Hegel (as Althusser has urged)[7] is an important question; but whatever the answer, Marx's use of dialectics to fashion his vision of history is hardly to be disputed. Marx's application of dialectics to society and history first appeared appropriately enough in his 'Introduction to the Critique of Hegel's Philosophy of Law', an article written in March–August 1843. It was here that the concept of a major contradiction in society, the contradiction of classes, was identified. The struggle it gave rise to must result in 'part of civil society emancipating itself and attaining universal supremacy'.[8] In Marx's and Engels's joint work *The Holy Family*, written the following year, and published in 1845, the relationship between 'the proletariat and [men of] wealth' is presented as one of 'antitheses',[9] and Engels in a speech in 1845 spoke of this as a 'contradiction which will develop more and more sharply'.[10]

In *The German Ideology* (1845–46), the next step was taken of sketching a succession of major classes based on different 'property relations', the development from one social formation to another taking place as a result of class struggle. Here it is assumed that human society from the very beginning had a form of 'division of labour', giving rise to a corresponding form of 'property'. As the division of labour become more and more complex, the forms of property changed, giving rise to corresponding classes, with mutually antagonistic interests. Thus, first, there was 'tribal property' with patriarchal relations growing into slavery; then 'ancient communal and state property' where 'the class relations between citizens and

---

[6] *Capital*, I, translated by S. Moore and E. Aveling, edited by F. Engels, London 1889, photographic reprint, edited by Dona Torr, London, 1938, pp. xxx–xxxi. All references to *Capital* are from this edition unless otherwise specified.

[7] Althusser, *For Marx*, pp. 89–116, 203–04, etc.

[8] For a summary and analysis of this article, of signal importance in the development of Marx's thought, see David McLellan, *Marx Before Marxism*, London 1980, pp. 142–57. The quoted words are given on p. 152.

[9] *Collected Works*, V, pp. 35–36.

[10] Ibid., p. 224.

slaves are now completely developed'. The third form was 'feudal or estate property', which had 'landowners' on one side and 'the enserfed small peasantry' on the other.[11] From out of these relationships developed the system of manufactures; and then, with large scale industry, came the modern 'bourgeois society', with possessors of 'industrial capital' being confronted by 'the proletarians'.[12]

It was clearly this understanding of the past attained within some five or six years by Marx and Engels that found its ultimate generalization in the sentence with which the main text of the *Manifesto* begins: 'The history of all hitherto existing society is the history of class struggles.'Despite such modification of the words 'all hitherto existing society' that Marx and Engels were to make later, this sentence undoubtedly represents the core of the materialist conception of history, and the basic premise on which any Marxist historiography can be constructed.

III

The reason why Marx and Engels came later to restrict the application of classes and class struggles to only the later (or historical) periods of 'all hitherto existing society' was because zoological science and social anthropology, which had seemingly lagged behind the progress of philosophy and political economy, made up the lag in the period following the *Manifesto*. In *The German Ideology* it had been assumed by Marx and Engels that the appearance of mankind, the formation of society and the division of labour were all inseparable and simultaneous events. Natural scientists had not as yet seen any evolutionary sequence in the origins of the various species, including *homo sapiens*; and there was yet no answer to the assertion that man, with his specific anatomical structure, was created all at once. In his Paris Manuscripts of 1844, Marx had found it easier to refute the conception of the creation of the world, by bringing up the results of geological observation, which pointed to spontaneous evolution. But

---

[11] *Collected Works*, V, pp. 32–36.
[12] *Collected Works*, V, pp. 66–89; *The German Ideology*, translated by Ryazanskaya, pp. 66–85.

for human evolution at the anatomical plane, there was nothing that Marx could urge, except to assert vehemently the fact of man's 'self-creation, his own formation process';[13] but this, on the basis of knowledge then available, could be valid only for the social, not anatomical, history of man. The current scientific belief still relied on the dictum of the immutability of each species that had been so authoritatively pronounced by Linnaeus (d.1778).

The scientific breakthrough came with the publication of Charles Darwin's *Origin of Species* in 1859. Evolution (and, therefore, dialectics) was at work even in the anatomical formation of man; and, no wonder, Marx was extremely excited by Darwin's great discovery.[14] This immediately opened the question of the transition from ape to man (on which Engels was to write a pamphlet in 1876),[15] and the nature of the evolution of society. In his 1844 Paris Manuscripts Marx had distinguished man from animals by his ability to produce more than what he immediately needed;[16] but now this capacity could also be seen as an acquired one after man had anatomically evolved.

The solution, for Marx and Engels, came to hand, when in 1877 the American anthropologist Lewis H. Morgan published his *Ancient Society, or Researches in the Lines of Human Progress from Savagery through Barbarism to Civilization*. Marx took copious notes from the book, though death (1883) prevented him from critically evaluating the results of Morgan's researches. But Engels carried out the required undertaking and published his *Origin of the Family, Private Property and the State* in 1884. In the Morganian state of 'savagery', human society existed, with production 'essentially collective'; the producers being also the consumers. The 'division of labour' came late, and, as it evolved, generated classes, until 'with slavery, which reached its fullest development in civilization, came the first great development

---

[13] See McLellan, *Marx Before Marxism*, pp. 190–91.
[14] Marx wrote to Lassalle (16 January 1861): 'Darwin's book is very important and serves me as a natural scientific basis for the class struggle in history.... Despite all deficiencies, not only is the death-blow dealt here for the first time to 'teleology' in the natural sciences, but its rational meaning is empirically explained'. Marx and Engels, *Selected Correspondence*, Moscow 1956, p. 151.
[15] *The Part Played by Labour in the Transition from Ape to Man*, Moscow 1949.
[16] McLellan, *Marx Before Marxism*, pp. 171–72.

of society into an exploiting and an exploited class'.[17] Classes and class struggles thus originated at a late stage in the time-span of human existence, when man could produce, and, therefore, be forced to produce, a surplus – and this the exploiting class could seize.

Once this decisive elucidation of the origin of class divisions in human society had been made, it became necessary for Engels to introduce a note in the 1888 English edition of the *Manifesto* to the effect that the phrase 'all hitherto existing society' should be modified to cover only the period of 'written history'. Since writing in all societies originated long after the ages of 'savagery' and 'barbarism' were past, this was a good counsel of caution. But Engels's note made it clear that what he wished to exclude was not the entire period previous to written history (now generally called prehistory), but the period of 'the primitive communistic society' when owing to the low level of production and collective organization, classes did not exist. Only when the primitive society decayed, did 'separate and finally antagonistic classes' appear on the scene.

IV

In its short description of the pre-modern classes, based mainly on European history, the *Manifesto* follows the longer description attempted in *The German Ideology*, already mentioned.[18] It particularly underlines two important points, both relating to the nature of class struggle in pre-modern epochs.

First, the class struggle though 'uninterrupted', was 'now hidden, now open'. In other words, since class interests were always in contradiction, class conflict was always present. But the extent to which the struggle was grasped as a class struggle in the contestants' consciousness varied: this seems the best way of how the words 'now hidden, now open' are to be understood. Here a passage in *The German*

---

[17] Engels, *The Origin of the Family, Private Property and the State*, Moscow 1948, pp. 247–50, to be read with the Preface to the first edition (pp. 13–14).

[18] One can compare the passages in the *Manifesto* with the detailed description of forms of property and corresponding classes in *The German Ideology, Collected Works*, V, pp. 32–35; *The German Ideology*, translated by Ryazanskaya, pp. 32–36.

Ideology may again be taken to have presaged more explicitly what the *Manifesto* here touches on, with rather tantalizing brevity:

> . . . all struggles within the state, the struggle between democracy, aristocracy, and monarchy, the struggle for the franchise, etc., etc., are mere illusory forms – altogether the general interest is the illusory form of common interests – in which the real struggles of the different classes are fought out among one another.[19]

In other words, written records of the past cannot, of themselves, always be expected to give a direct explicit exposition of the class struggles as were then taking place. Marx was to note in his Preface to *A Contribution to the Critique of Political Economy* that a period of social transformation cannot be judged 'by its own consciousness' in the same way as 'one does not judge an individual by what he says about himself'.[20] One major change from earlier times brought about by the rise of capitalism is that the oppressed class, the proletariat, is becoming more and more conscious of its own existence as a class and of the fundamental antagonism between itself and the owners of capital.

The second feature of pre-capitalist formations that the *Manifesto* mentions, explains why the class struggle could so often remain dormant in the consciousness of the oppressed classes. This was because of the complexity of those earlier class structures:

> In the earlier epochs of history, we find almost everywhere a complicated arrangement of society into various orders, a manifold gradations of social rank. In ancient Rome we have patricians, knights, plebeians, slaves; in the Middle Ages, feudal lords, vassals, guild masters, journeymen, apprentices, serfs; in almost all of these classes, again, subordinate gradations.

In *The German Ideology* Marx and Engels had already explained

---

[19] *Collected Works*, V, pp. 46–47; *The German Ideology*, translated by Ryazanskaya, p. 45.
[20] *A Contribution to the Critique of Political Economy*, p. 21.

how such complexities in medieval Europe hindered the development of class struggle.[21] In that text a further important point was made, that such complexity was to be expected in all societies where human relations were based not purely on exchange, but on custom and other social institutions ('personal relations'). But things change, when, as in modern bourgeois society, individuals are 'independent of one another and are only held together by exchange'. Here as labour (or, as Marx would say later, labour power) itself becomes a commodity, in conditions of 'large-scale industry', the class contradictions become overwhelmingly dominant and sharper.[22]

This conclusion is repeated in more vibrant language in the *Manifesto*:

> Our epoch, the epoch of the bourgeoisie, possesses, however, this distinctive feature: it has simplified the class antagonisms. Society as a whole is more and more splitting into two great classes directly facing each other: Bourgeoisie and Proletariat.

These ideas about the nature of class structures and class struggles were offered in the *Manifesto* in respect of Europe, to which till then the knowledge of Marx and Engels had been largely restricted. But in the 1850s Marx began to read extensively about India, and it clearly seemed to him that the caste system was another form of those complex gradations which had marked pre-bourgeois societies in Europe. Writing in 1853 he saw that the foundations of the caste system lay in 'hereditary divisions of labour', divisions that, as he noted later, were carried to the extreme of 'conversion of fractional work into the life-calling of one man'. By their divisiveness, the castes constituted 'decisive impediments to Indian progress and Indian power'. Yet these divisions, like the pre-modern gradations in Europe touched upon in the *Manifesto*, could not withstand the introduction of bourgeois conditions: 'Modern industry, resulting from the railway sys-

---

[21] *Collected Works*, V, pp. 64–66; *The German Ideology*, translated by Ryazanskaya, pp. 64–66.

[22] *Collected Works*, V, pp. 63–64; passage not traceable in Ryazanskaya's translation.

tem will dissolve the hereditary divisions of labour, upon which rest the Indian castes . . .'.[23]

Marx might have been optimistic here, and did not allow for the continuing ideological backwardness which would sustain the caste system, even after its main economic basis in the form of division of labour had been removed or curtailed. But what is important for us is that within almost five years of composing the *Manifesto*, he was essentially recognizing a prospective historical process in India similar to the one that had taken place in Europe – a complex of class gradations being immensely simplified by the onset of capitalist relations. Here, therefore, there was no desire in Marx to seek any exceptionalism for areas outside Europe.

V

It will be noticed that in the *Manifesto* there is not yet any use of the term 'mode of production'. The term with its sense definitely established occurs in the *Grundrisse*, Marx's extensive manuscript notes, composed in 1857–58;[24] but the *locus classicus* for the term is the Preface to *A Contribution to the Critique of Political Economy*, which Marx published early in 1859 immediately after *Grundrisse*. In the Preface the 'mode of production' appears as the sum total of 'the relations of production' – the base – and the 'legal and political institutions' and 'forms of social consciousness' which correspond to it. A 'mode of production' having passed its prime begins to decay from its own contradictions, whereafter 'an era of social revolution' ensues, leading to the rise of new 'superior relations of production'. And so 'in broad outline' Marx could distinguish 'the Asiatic, ancient, feudal and bourgeois modes of production' as successive social formations.[25]

It could be said that the succession of ancient, feudal, and bour-

---

[23] 'The Future Results of British Rule in India' (*New York Daily Tribune*, 8 August 1853), in Marx and Engels, *On Colonialism*, Moscow 1976, p. 85. The reference to division carried to fractional work is from *Capital*, I, p. 331.

[24] See *Grundrisse*, translated by Martin Nicolaus, Harmondsworth 1973, p. 495 (Marx, *Pre-capitalist Economic Formations*, translated by Jack Cohen, edited by E.J. Hobsbawm, pp. 94–95), for possibly the first occurrence of the term, with a clear indication of sense.

[25] *A Contribution to the Critique of Political Economy*, pp. 20–22.

geois modes, with slave, serf and wage-labour as the respective defin-
ing basic forms of relations of production, is implied in the text of the
Manifesto (and in the earlier *German Ideology*), as we have seen. Essentially, what the Preface to the *Critique* does, is to put that description into a more theoretically refined mould, through a clearer
application of the dialectical method to social history.

The reference to the Asiatic mode is, however, one singular addition, since there is no trace of it in the *Manifesto* or earlier writings.
Marx and Engels appear to have become interested in the economic
formations outside Europe for the first time in 1853; and there is much
reflection in the *Grundrisse* (1857–58) on the Indian ('Asiatic')
community and the despotic states that arose to exploit these communities.[26] When Marx listed the 'Asiatic' as the earliest mode, preceding the ancient and feudal, he probably had in mind not a territorial
mode but the earliest form of 'tribal property' which he thought lasted
in Asia much longer than in Europe. This becomes clear from his
statement in the *Grundrisse* that

> Slavery and serfdom are thus only further developments of the
> form of property resting on the clan system. They necessarily
> modified all of the latter's forms. They can do this least of all in
> the Asiatic form.[27]

The intrusion of the 'Asiatic' in a succession of 'modes' was not
without its problems, especially since its persistence would imply, as
Marx rather incautiously stated in 1853, that

> Indian society has no history at all, at least no known history.
> What we call its history is the history of successive intruders who
> founded their empires on the basis of that unresisting and un-
> changing society.[28]

Clearly, the emergence of individual petty production within the

---

[26] *Grundrisse*, pp. 473–86; *Pre-capitalist Economic Formations*, pp. 70–82.
[27] *Grundrisse*, p. 493; *Pre-capitalist Economic Formations*, p. 91.
[28] 'Future Results of British Rule', *On Colonialism*, p. 81.

community, the production of a marketable surplus and so the emergence of a commodity sector along with the presumed 'natural' economy of the village, the appearance of a 'despotic' power, taking 'rent' as 'tax', processes recognized by Marx himself as taking shape within the 'Asiatic' system, meant that the Asian continent, or India (to Marx, the main ground for his 'Asiatic' evidence), could not be devoid of historical change.[29] One should moreover remember that the denial of history to India, expressed in 1853, was never repeated by Marx and Engels; and that, while in 1888 Engels did suggest a modification to the 'history of class struggles' formulation in the *Manifesto* in order to accommodate the stage of primitive communism, he proposed no further modification in order to provide for the history-less 'Asiatic Mode'. There is, therefore, no doubt the universality of the *Manifesto's* principal historical dictum about class struggle continued to be upheld by its authors, as applying to all societies blessed by the exploitation of one class by another (as the 'Asiatic' mode in its 'despotic' form certainly was). There could be no exceptions to this rule.[30]

VI

The *Manifesto* provides us with a sketch of the emergence and development of the bourgeoisie, tracing its origins to 'the serfs of the Middle Ages', from amongst whom 'sprang the chartered burghers', from whom, in turn, came 'the first elements of the bourgeoisie'. In Marx's usage the terms 'bourgeoisie' and 'capitalists' are not always synonymous. 'Bourgeoisie' is generally the broader term, representing not only the owners of capital, who employ wage-labour in modern industry – and to whom he restricts the term 'capitalist' in *Capital* – but is a much larger class with much earlier origins, and includes mer-

---

[29] I venture to refer to my own detailed discussion of problems in Marx's changing perceptions of the Asiatic Mode in 'Marx's Perception of India', *Essays in Indian History: Towards a Marxist Perception*, New Delhi 1995, pp. 16–35.

[30] But see Hobsbawm, who attributes the view to Marx that 'the Asiatic society' is 'not yet a class society, or if it is a class society, then it is the [its?] most primitive form'. Introduction to *Pre-Capitalist Economic Formations*, p. 34. There are no statements in Marx and Engels to support this extreme inference.

chants, and pre-industrial manufacturers, from whose fold 'the modern bourgeois', the industrial capitalists proper, have arisen.

The *Manifesto* identifies two important factors for the rise of the bourgeoisie and the emergence of capitalism. The first was the growth of the market, initiated by the discovery of America and the rounding of the Cape of Good Hope, which resulted in Europe's access to the 'East-Indian and Chinese markets, the colonization of America, [and] trade with the colonies . . .'. These markets required production on a scale for which the feudal craft-guild system was unsuitable; large workshops had, therefore, to be established, with 'division of labour' not, as previously, between guilds but within 'each single workshop': this was the basis of 'the manufacturing system', which was ultimately dissolved or transformed by machinery into the modern factory system.

This account was based on Marx's and Engels's economic and historical studies, carried on till that date. The relationship of market to production was at the heart of the great controversy between the Mercantilists and their opponents, out of which controversy the science of Political Economy originated. The increase in productivity caused by the division of labour within the workshop had been classically emphasized by Adam Smith in 1776.[31] And the transformation wrought by machinery was especially studied by Ricardo in a new chapter added to his text in 1821.[32] Marx had already discussed in his *Poverty of Philosophy* (1847) the matter of the markets ('the increase of commodities put into circulation from the moment trade penetrated to the East Indies, by way of the Cape of Good Hope; the colonial system; the development of maritime trade'), of the 'workshop' of the 'manufacturing industry', and of the transformation in the division of labour brought about by machinery;[33] what the *Manifesto* does is to reproduce the essential points made there.

But, if the *Manifesto* sums up what classical Political Economy

---

[31] *An Inquiry into the Nature and Cause of the Wealth of Nations*, I, London 1910, pp. 4–11.

[32] David Ricardo, *The Principles of Political Economy and Taxation*, London 1911, pp. 263–71 (Chapter XXXI, 'On Machinery').

[33] *Collected Works*, VI, pp. 184–87; *The Poverty of Philosophy*, Moscow n.d., pp. 151–57.

had already expounded with regard to the growth of bourgeois relations of production, it necessarily lacked what came to be Marx's own
crucial contribution to the history of capitalism, viz. the theory of the
primitive or primary accumulation of capital. In 1857–58 in the
Grundrisse Marx made some important observations about 'the original accumulation of capital', but this was done mainly in order to
show that not money, but social changes, helped to bring such accumulation about.[34] These remarks can hardly be considered to antici-
pate the main theory that was presented in all its fullness in the last
portion of *Capital*, Volume I, Part VIII: 'The So-called Primitive Accumulation'.[35]

Marx here begins by pointing out that the initial circuit of capitalist production can take place only when possessors of capital and
free labourers can come together 'face to face'. This is made possible
only if the former have accumulated wealth (convertible into capital)
outside of, or previous to, capitalist production, and the latter have
been 'freed' of their means of production as petty producers. There
must therefore be a process of 'expropriation' of the one class by the
other before capitalist production can begin. It is this process that
constitutes 'Primitive Accumulation'.[36]

Marx describes two such major processes or forms of primitive
accumulation: one, internal; the other, external. Taking England as
the classical case he describes at length how the English peasant was
deprived of his land, from the period of the Tudor enclosures to the
private and parliamentary enclosures of the eighteenth century.[37]
Primitive accumulation here was achieved by brute force, its principal
moments those when

> great masses of men are suddenly and forcibly torn from their
> means of subsistence, and hurled as free and 'unattached' prole-

---

[34] *Grundrisse*, pp. 259, 506–10.

[35] *Capital*, I, pp. 736–800. It is, perhaps possible that 'primary' may be a better
rendering than 'primitive' as in Eden and Cedar Paul's translation of *Capital*, I,
London 1951, II, p. 790. But since 'primitive' is authorized by Engels, who
supervised the Moore–Aveling translation, and has been in general use, it seems
better to stick to it here.

[36] *Capital*, I, pp. 736–39.

[37] Ibid., pp. 740–57.

tarians on the labour market. The expropriation of the agricultural producer, from the soil, is the basis of the whole process.[38]

The second process, the external, consisted of the forcible plunder
and expropriation of colonial peoples:

> The discovery of gold and silver in America, the extirpation, en-
> slavement and entombment in mines of the aboriginal [Amerin-
> dian] population, the beginning of the conquest and looting of
> the East Indies, the turning of Africa into a warren for the com-
> mercial hunting of black skins, signalized the rosy dawn of the
> era of capitalist production. These idyllic proceedings are the chief
> momenta of primitive accumulation.[39]

Of these proceedings Marx then offers a trenchant account, touching
on the colonial regimes of terror, the loot of India, the slaughter of
the Amerindian people and, not the least, the African slave trade.[40]

This picture of the rise of capitalism is profoundly different from
that given in the *Manifesto*, where we see burgesses growing into
modern bourgeois by simple expansion of trade and gains from production. But Marx now dismisses this simple mode of growth
(transformation of guild-masters and artisans into 'full-blown capitalists' through 'gradually extending exploitation of wage-labour and
corresponding accumulation') as a process that would have given only
'snail's pace' to the development of capitalist production.[41] Primitive
accumulation, forcible expropriation, internal and external, could
alone give the necessary pace and scale to capital accumulation. Force
was central to this process – the whole process of primitive accumulation illustrated how 'force is the midwife of every old society, preg-
nant with a new one. It is in itself an economic power.'[42]

One must, therefore, realise that the description of the rise of
capitalism in the *Manifesto* is seriously incomplete. The forcible

[38] Ibid., p. 739.
[39] Ibid., p. 775.
[40] Ibid., pp. 775–78, 784–85.
[41] Ibid., p. 774.
[42] Ibid., p. 776.

expropriation of the peasants and colonial peoples (as against simple conquests of rural and colonial markets) do not appear in the *Manifesto*: even the infamous trans-Atlantic slave trade is not mentioned. This was because, as we have seen, the *Manifesto* had basically accepted what classical Political Economy had till then taught about the growth of production through an expansion of the market and forms of division of labour. Marx subsequently made his own historical discoveries, leading to another decisive break (comparable to the one in the realm of surplus value) from the legacy of Adam Smith and Ricardo.

VII

At the time of the drafting of the *Manifesto*, Marx was well aware of the effect of England's industrial development on crafts and employment in non-capitalist countries. In 1845–46, he and Engels noted in *The German Ideology* how 'if in England a machine is invented [it] deprives countless workers of bread in India and China'.[43] A year later in the *Poverty of Philosophy*, while speaking of economists' optimism with regard to 'improvement', Marx asked sarcastically whether they 'were thinking of the millions of workers who had to perish in the East Indies so as to procure for the million and half workers employed in the same [textile] industry in England three years' prosperity out of ten'.[44]

These statements are not repeated in the *Manifesto*, though it does say that 'all old established national industries have been destroyed or are being destroyed', where the authors might have had in mind colonial craft industries as well. Then follows a passage which touches upon the new condition of dependence that capitalism was imposing on the rest of the world:

> Just as it [the bourgeoisie] has made the country dependent on the towns, so it has made barbarian and semi-barbarian coun-

---

[43] *Collected Works*, V, p. 51; *The German Ideology*, translated by Ryazanskaya, p. 60.

[44] *Collected Works*, VI, p. 160; *The Poverty of Philosophy*, p. 113.

tries dependent on the civilized ones, nations of peasants on nations of bourgeois, the East on the West.

It should be recognized that this dependence is visualized in the
Manifesto in economic terms, not political. 'The prices of its commodities', it says a few lines earlier, 'are the heavy artillery with which
it [the bourgeoisie] batters down all Chinese walls, with which it forces
the barbarians' intensely obstinate hatred of foreigners to capitulate'.
Yet as Marx was himself later to note, it had been not cheap prices,
but canon with which Britain forced China to open its markets to
opium and other goods through the infamous First Opium War, 1840–
42.[45]

In a very important (but rather neglected) article of 1859 Marx
noted that Chinese goods could not be undersold by British exports
because Britain did not yet have the necessary political power in China
to undermine the position of Chinese rural producers, in the way it
had done in India.[46] And with respect to India, Marx had seen as
early as 1853 that the Free Traders needed first to conquer it ('to get
it') 'in order to subject it to their sharp philanthropy'.[47] In 1859, again,
he remarked on the financial burdens England had to accept 'for the
"glorious" reconquest of India' after the 1857 Revolt, for the purpose
of 'securing the monopoly of the Indian market to the Manchester
free traders'.[48] It nearly seems as if Marx was anticipating the notion
of imperialism of free trade, which Gallagher and Robinson introduced
in a seminal article published almost a hundred years later, in 1953.[49]
In general, Marx's attitude towards colonialism hardened perceptibly
as he read more about it. One can see from his articles in the *New*

---

[45] In 1853 Marx spoke of 'British canon forcing [opium] on China', *New York
Daily Tribune (NYDT)*, 14 June 1853, *On Colonialism*, p. 19.

[46] *NYDT*, 3 December 1859; *Collected Works*, XVI, p. 539. For some reason this
article is not included in *On Colonialism*.

[47] *NYDT*, 11 July 1853; *On Colonialism*, p. 49.

[48] *NYDT*, 30 April 1859; *Collected Works*, XVI, p. 286; omitted in *On Colonialism*.

[49] John Gallagher and Ronald Robinson, 'The Imperialism of Free Trade', *Economic
History Review*, second series, VI, 1953, pp. 1–15.

York Daily Tribune in the 1850s what harsh and uncompromising indictment of the colonial system he was capable of.[50]

Since the *Manifesto* precedes its authors' attainment of the recognition of colonialism as a necessary adjunct of free trade, it naturally does not put forward any explicit objective of colonial emancipation. But within very few years of its publication, Marx himself was savouring the prospect of a free China and free India. In 1850 he closed a report on China with the words:

> When in their imminent flight across Asia our European reactionaries will ultimately arrive at the Wall of China, . . . who knows if they will not find there the inscription: 'The Chinese Republic – Liberty, Equality, Fraternity.'[51]

And three years later, he was looking forward to 'the Hindus [Indians] [having] grown strong enough to throw off the English yoke altogether'.[52]

VIII

The Communist Manifesto was written to meet an important need – the need to put in a short text the main principles of Communism, a task that was brilliantly performed – the stirring language conveying the main ideas without loss of precision. If the *Manifesto* was written in time to offer to the proletariat a guide before it entered the revolutionary upsurge of Europe in 1848, its value has only grown further in that today, after the grave retreat of socialism on the world scale in the last decade and more, the working class of all countries needs to be rallied to the cause of socialism still more urgently and more resolutely. But these very circumstances also require that

---

[50] The two major collections of these articles are *On Colonialism*, used in this paper, and Shlomo Avineri (ed.), *Karl Marx on Colonialism and Modernization*, New York 1969; the latter is the more extensive collection. The volumes of the *Collected Works* are not only the most comprehensive in their coverage, but have the most accurate texts as well.

[51] *Neue Rheinische Zeitung*, No.2 (1850); *On Colonialism*, p. 18.

[52] *NYDT*, 8 August 1853; *On Colonialism*, p. 85.

Marxian theory should be closely and critically grasped. One needs, therefore, to look at the *Manifesto's* contents carefully in the light of the stage in the evolution of Marxism at which it was written. The perception of historical development, especially of the development of capitalism, was considerably enriched by Marx and Engels in the years after the publication of the *Manifesto*. The present paper is an attempt to indicate in what areas we must supplement the theoretical framework of the *Manifesto* by drawing upon the later discoveries and insights of its authors. A reading of the *Manifesto*, with these kept in mind, can surely help us to serve its cause only still better.

Prabhat Patnaik

The Communist Manifesto
After 150 Years

The Communist Manifesto

was the first systematic attempt in published form at an exposition of
the Marxist world outlook. Both Marx and Engels had been moving
towards the development of this outlook for some years, though along
different routes: Marx through his manuscript *Contribution to the
Critique of Hegel's Philosophy of Law* (1843, first published in 1927),
and Engels through his book *The Condition of the Working Class in
England in 1844* (1845). By 1845 they had given its basic outline in
their jointly authored work *The German Ideology*, though this was
never published during their lifetime. *The Poverty of Philosophy*, published a few months before *The Communist Manifesto*, did contain
some of their conclusions, but it was a polemic against Proudhon and

not a systematic exposition of their own ideas. *The Communist Manifesto* thus represented the first public exposition of their world outlook. Since it was a manifesto, the exposition had to be short, pithy, and oriented towards praxis. Its impact was all the more powerful as a consequence.

The *Manifesto* expounded above all the materialist conception of history, and this, in the form in which it appeared in the *Manifesto*, had four distinguishing features: first, it recognized an inner dynamics in history and located the source of this movement in the dialectics of the interplay between the social productive forces and the social relations of production, of which the property relations were the most decisive constituent. Secondly, it showed how this dialectics was realized through the agency of social classes and class-struggles. Thirdly, it specifically analysed in a brief but comprehensive fashion how this dialectics was manifesting itself in the historical evolution of the capitalist mode of production. And finally, it explained why capitalism was the last antagonistic mode of production, how it created the special historical agency, the proletariat, that would bring about the transcendence not only of capitalism itself but of all class exploitation, and take mankind from its 'pre-history' to its 'history'.

To be sure, these perceptions of Marx and Engels were not without their lineages. The 'spectre of Communism', it should be remembered, was already 'haunting' Europe when *The Communist Manifesto* was first published in February 1848. Many of its ideas in rudimentary form had already been in circulation. Babeuf, for instance, had talked of communism a half-century before the *Manifesto*. The Scottish historical school (Ferguson, Millar), not to mention Saint-Simon, had put forward certain basic ideas of historical materialism. Lorenz von Stein had propounded the conception of the proletariat as the major historical force in modern society. Indeed by their own admission, Karl Marx and Frederick Engels were not the originators of these ideas.

The *Manifesto* however stood out for three reasons. First, its young authors brought together these particular insights into one dazzling theoretical structure, which not only gave precision and rigour to each of these insights, but also infused immense power into the whole. In particular, the rigorous presentation of the materialist conception of history, which made history an object of analysis rather than a sequence of episodes and personalities, was captivating. Secondly, they postulated a denouement to the saga of class struggle through history, in the form of a social revolution where the proletariat organizes itself as a ruling class in order to end all class rule. (This was to be called the 'dictatorship of the proletariat' later). Thirdly, and most importantly, they argued that the objective condition for this denouement to be realized was being created by bourgeois society itself by the working of its own immanent laws. It was creating a situation, for the first time in human history, where not only was the primary oppressed class the most consistently revolutionary and energetic class, but it also had no specific class interests of its own, opposed to those of the other oppressed classes. While earlier class struggles between the oppressors and the oppressed had given birth to new antagonistic formations, the class struggle in bourgeois society was the prelude to the end of all antagonism.

This was because of the operation of two distinct tendencies in bourgeois society: first, its tendency towards universalizing itself through a destruction of all other modes of production and the reduction of all other classes, including sections of the bourgeoisie itself, to the status of proletarians; and secondly, its tendency to concentrate the proletarians into larger and larger masses with the growth of modern industry, endowing them objectively with a capacity for collective action. Once bourgeois society has got established, the only way forward for history then is for its objects, the proletarians, to assume the role of self-conscious subjects, and in this role to bring about the end of history as we know it till now.

This vision gave the *Manifesto* immense appeal. Many previous theories had dreamt of a 'moral order', a society free from class exploitation. Marx and Engels not only postulated the historical inevitability of a 'moral order', a classless society, but also argued that the objective condition for this historical transition had actually arrived. The *Manifesto*, in other words, actualized the revolution; it charted a path leading from today to the 'first step in the revolution', which is 'to raise the proletariat to the position of the ruling class', and even beyond. It meant therefore a decisive break from all forms of utopian socialism. And it vastly enhanced the appeal of socialism by converting it from a mere dream to an imminently realizable historical project. It did not eschew the moral–ethical foundations of socialism; it located them in this very historical process that was moving towards a denouement.

II

The *Manifesto*, however, bore in several ways the imprint of its immediate context, namely the revolutionary situation in Europe. The audience it addressed itself to was a limited one; the revolution it visualized was a pure proletarian revolution; the mode of production which its analysis focused on was capitalism; and the capitalism it analysed was a 'closed' system, where the colonies and the empires did not figure. To be sure, Europe was having a spate of workers' uprisings (including one a few days after the *Manifesto's* publication), and Marx and Engels were not writing a tome but a manifesto in preparation for what was then seen as the coming revolution. But this vision which shaped the way the *Manifesto* achieved the unity between its grand theory and its specific perception of praxis, and which gave its appeal strength, also constituted its limitation.

The fact that the *Manifesto's* concrete concern covered only a limited terrain, and that it represented therefore only a first step, though a momentous one, is obvious. The 'Communists of various nationalities' who had assembled in London to adopt the *Manifesto* were supposed to have it published 'in the English, French, German, Italian, Flemish and Danish languages'. The *Manifesto*, notwithstanding a reference to the United States, was addressed essentially to Europe. Moreover, it was addressed not even to the whole of Europe, but only to Western Europe where the four big countries were Germany, England, France and Italy. As it happens, the proposed translations of the *Manifesto* to all these languages did not even materialize according to plan: the English translation, for instance, had to wait till 1888, a full forty years after the original publication. But even the concern of the *Manifesto* was narrow: let alone the vast expanse of colonies, semi-colonies, dependencies and other 'Third World' countries, it did not even stretch to Russia.

The narrowness of this concern reflected two things: first, Marx's analysis of capitalism had still not been carried to the point where its interaction with pre-capitalist modes, as in the colonies, or its appearance in the form of a backward capitalism, as in Russia, could be theoretically comprehended. Secondly, as a consequence, the conception of revolution was still confined to a pure proletarian revolution (achieved no doubt through diverse routes) in the advanced capitalist countries. In other words, the theory had yet to acquire the breadth and depth that Marx himself was to impart to it shortly afterwards, not to mention later Marxists. By 1853, i.e., within five years of the *Manifesto*, Marx was coming to grips with the colonial situation of India, through his *New York Daily Tribune* articles, and visualizing the possibility of 'the Hindoos themselves' becoming 'strong enough to throw off the English yoke altogether' even before a situation arises in Great Britain where 'the now ruling classes' are 'supplanted by the industrial proletariat'. Likewise, as Marxist ideas spread rapidly in Russia in the 1870s after the publication of *Capital*, volume 1, in Russian translation, Marx and Engels entertained hopes of a Russian revolution in the late 1870s. Marx even inclined towards the view that the Russian village community could provide the basis for a transition to socialism, if supported by a socialist revolution in Western Europe, without having to undergo prior disintegration through capitalist development. Marx sought to justify this view in his famous letter to Vera Zasulich in 1881, though Russian Marxists rejected it and Engels later withdrew from it even while continuing to hope for a Russian revolution that would give 'the signal for the workers' revolution in the West, so that both supplement each other'. Marx's increasing interest in Russian and non-European societies not only enriched his analysis of capitalism but contributed greatly to the expansion of the terrain over which historical materialism was applied.

Likewise, bourgeois society was seen in the *Manifesto* as a 'closed' society, in isolation from colonies, from imperialism, from the international economy (including inter-capitalist relations). This may be explained by the authors' immediate project, but the failure of that project owed precisely to the factors on which the *Manifesto* was silent. The international relations in which capitalism was enmeshed played a major role in belying the *Manifesto* prognostications about a

European proletarian revolution. The period from the mid-nineteenth century till the First World War (when according to Hobsbawm the 'long nineteenth century' ended[1]) was one of a very pronounced boom, in the course of which the European working class did experience some improvement in its living standards (though these still continued to be pretty miserable). This prolonged boom was made possible by the 'drain' of surplus from colonies like India, and the availability of their markets 'on tap', which played an important role in sustaining the Gold Standard, and in financing British capital exports to the temperate regions of white settlement, like Australia, Canada, and the United States.[2] Together with capital exports there was a massive migration of European workers (about fifty million during the nineteenth century) to these regions, the so-called 'empty spaces', which kept down the potential social explosion that Marx had anticipated as a sequel to growing unemployment.

Marx and Engels became sensitive to this very soon. By the early 1850s, as mentioned earlier, Marx was not only writing about British colonialism in India but even visualizing the possibility of an uprising in India even before a workers' revolution in Britain. And Engels, as early as 1858, just ten years after the *Manifesto*, was seeing a connection between England's exploitation of the whole world and the fact that the 'English proletariat is becoming more and more bourgeois'. But the *Manifesto* itself does not reflect any of this thinking. The unified theory of the *Manifesto* (including its perception of praxis) therefore was barren in terms of its revolutionary outcome. It was only the recreation of a new unified theory more than half a century later by Lenin, reflecting an altogether new phase of capitalism and putting imperialism at the centre of analysis, which provided a fresh basis for a revolutionary advance.

---

[1] E.J. Hobsbawm, *The Age of Extremes*, London 1995.

[2] S.B. Saul, *Studies in British Overseas Trade*, Liverpool 1970, is the classic reference on this. See also A.K. Bagchi, 'Some International Foundations of Capitalist Growth and Underdevelopment', *Economic and Political Weekly*, Special Number, August 1972. I have dwelt on this argument at length in my *Accumulation and Stability Under Capitalism*, Oxford 1997, Chapter 11.

The hallmark of the new unified theory of Lenin was that it universal-ized its vision of the revolution, giving priority neither to the prole-tariat in the metropolis nor to the workers and peasants in the colonies. The fact that imperialism emerges with the completion of the parti-tioning of the world among the major capitalist powers, so that the whole world in a sense is knit together, with developments in any part affecting all other parts, enabled Lenin to advance his theory of the 'weakest link'. Anti-imperialist struggles in the backward econo-mies and the proletarian struggles in the imperialist countries were dialectically related, and this era of revolutionary transformation that imperialism brought on the agenda could be triggered off wherever the chain had its weakest link. Within this perspective, and with the hopes of a German revolution receding, Lenin increasingly cast his eyes towards the East, and in one of his last articles wrote:

> In the last analysis the outcome of the struggle will be determined by the fact that Russia, India, China, etc., account for the over-whelming majority of the population of the globe. And during the past few years it is this majority that has been drawn into the struggle for emancipation with extraordinary rapidity, so that in this respect there cannot be the slightest doubt what the final outcome of the world struggle will be. In this sense, the complete victory of socialism is fully and absolutely assured.

Together with the enriching of the conception of the world revo-lutionary process beyond what the *Manifesto* had visualized, there was a parallel enriching of the conception of the stages of revolution. The *Manifesto* had already emphasized the diversity that existed even within Western Europe and the fact that different countries would be having different routes of transition to proletarian revolution. Ger-many for instance was supposed to be 'on the eve of a bourgeois revo-lution'. But this bourgeois revolution would be occurring with a much more developed proletariat than what England had in the seventeenth and France in the eighteenth century. Consequently the bourgeois revolution in Germany was supposed to be 'but the prelude to an immediately following proletarian revolution'. The routes that the different countries were to follow, in other words, were all leading essentially to proletarian revolutions. The *Manifesto* said little about the role of the peasantry in the revolution, or about the relationship between the proletariat and the peasantry, or about the fact that where the peasantry continued to be a significant social force, the transition to a proletarian revolution would have to be much more protracted. The bourgeois revolutions in such situations might not be brief, transient affairs, as the *Manifesto* visualized for Germany, but more or less prolonged stages. And, what is more, the bourgeoisie itself might not be able to carry through the bourgeois democratic revolution, in which case the proletariat, in alliance with the peasantry, would have to take upon itself the task of carrying through the democratic revolution long before any question of a proletarian revolution comes onto the agenda. These issues which were not very significant in the context of the advanced countries of Western Europe, became crucial once the entire globe was seen as providing a potential terrain of revolution in any part of it that constituted the 'weakest link'.

This parallel development of enriching the conception of the stages of revolution had of course begun with Engels' *The Peasant War in Germany*, but it was carried forward by the writings of Lenin (*Two Tactics of Social Democracy in the Democratic Revolution*), Mao Zedong (*New Democracy*), and the substantial theoretical work done by the Communist movement, especially in the Third World countries.

IV

These subsequent theoretical developments however also took off from the *Manifesto*. Lenin, for example, did not have to rediscover all over again the concepts of class struggle and historical materialism. Thus, while the limitations of the *Manifesto* arising from its particular context must be recognized, the distance travelled by the Communist movement since the *Manifesto* constitutes a tribute to the *Manifesto* itself, to the fact that it opened up a whole new world of revolutionary theory and practice.

It would be as erroneous then to claim that the subsequent development of Marxist theory was merely an unfolding of the insights presented in the *Manifesto*, as it would be to dismiss the *Manifesto* as 'Eurocentric' and hence of little more than of historical interest. The relation between the *Manifesto* and subsequent Marxist theory needs careful interpretation, and an excursus on this may be in order here.

The *Manifesto* talked of 'bourgeois ideologists who have raised themselves to the level of comprehending theoretically the historical movement as a whole'. Lenin referred to the fact that the coinciding of two phenomena, namely the emergence of the revolutionary proletariat, and the discovery of historical materialism, ensured that the two together constituted a decisive force in the transition of mankind from its pre-history to its history. An impression may be gathered from these remarks that a theoretical comprehension of the historical process is a once-for-all act, that once it has been achieved, it provides an understanding of every moment of history thenceforth, and creates an indissoluble unity of theory and praxis which from then on consciously takes mankind forward.

This, however, is an erroneous impression. The theoretical comprehension of the historical process is not a matter of 'revelation' or of 'acquiring enlightenment'. It represents a continuous effort to achieve comprehension, and the process is never complete. There are several reasons for this. First, the unfolding of the historical process itself takes novel directions which are not anticipated by the development of theory till then; secondly, even when the historical process unfolds in a manner which is in conformity with theory, the task of explicating this unfolding remains to be done; and thirdly, the theoretical comprehension provided by the existing Marxist analysis is itself incomplete even with regard to the past, let alone the present or the future. This last point about incompleteness does not just relate to the need for mere *additions* to the corpus of Marxist theory; it relates to the fact that this theory must be continuously reconstituted to take account of ever larger totalities.

Marxian theory, in other words, represents not a 'closed system', but a phenomenon that is in a continuous process of reconstitution. Even this continuous process of reconstitution does not necessarily make the theory complete at every moment of time. Significant incompletenesses remain and may do so for long stretches of time.

An example would make the point clear: despite all reconstitutions, there still remains a glaring incompleteness in Marxist theory which relates to the theory of imperialism. Lenin drew a distinction between colonialism and imperialism, seeing the latter as characterizing the monopoly phase of capitalism and as being superimposed upon, and making use of, the already existing colonial relations. But even Lenin did not go into the nature of these colonial relations themselves, and the role they play in the process of reproduction of capital. Since Marx's analysis, not just in the *Manifesto*, but even in *Capital*, is concerned essentially with a 'closed' capitalist economy, the interaction between capitalism and the colonies remains an area of silence for Marxist theory (apart from Luxemburg's solitary and incomplete effort). The problem here is not about what happened in history; indeed Marxist historians, especially from the Third World, have done invaluable work to throw light on this question. The problem is to incorporate it into the core of Marxist *theory*.

Such incorporation cannot be a mere 'add on', since the theory as it stands provides little room for any such 'add on'. After all Marx's consideration of capitalism as a 'closed' economy was not an oversight or a mere simplifying assumption. Once a 'mode of production' is conceptualized in terms of the appropriation of surplus value from the direct producers, and the capital–wage labour relationship is highlighted as constituting the essence of capitalism, then there is no obvious theoretical role left for colonies and pre-capitalist segments in the dynamics of capitalism (other than in the rudimentary stage of the primitive accumulation of capital). The 'drain' from them may add to the available surplus value, but it is not essential; pre-capitalist markets may help alleviate crises, but unless one believes that capitalism is an *incomplete* system where the sphere of realization is necessarily separated from the sphere of production (which Marx did not believe and which would generate further theoretical problems) there is again no necessary role for colonies.

The point of all this is to argue *not* that Marxian theory cannot be completed to take account of the problem of colonialism (my own inclination would be to introduce the idea of 'reserve markets' and 'reserve sources of raw materials' together with the 'reserve army of labour'), but that it is in need of a continuous process of completion, or rather of reconstitution which can never achieve either momentary or permanent finality. Any such reconstitution necessarily occurs around a core; and in the case of Marxism that core is to be found in the *Manifesto*.

To say this should not give the impression that there is a duality in the body of Marxist thought, between a core that is fixed for all time and a non-core that changes with every reconstitution of Marxism. The reconstitution cannot but leave its imprint on what one regards as the core itself, developing it, reshaping it and altering it, albeit at the margin. Nonetheless all reconstitution occurs on the basis of certain essential categories, and a certain cognition of relations between them, which are the hallmak of Marxism, and without which the reconstitution would forfeit all claims to being considered Marxist. These categories make their first appearance in the *Manifesto*, which thus provides the core for subsequent attempts at reconstitution. And the strength of Marxism at any time is judged by the validity of the reconstitution that has been undertaken.

This continuous reconstitution of Marxism, both for overcoming existing incompleteness and for comprehending unfolding history, is not only necessary, but is in fact what is occurring all the time, for otherwise Marxism would have been dead by now. In our own country, for example, the remarkable recent innovations introduced by the Communist movement in the form of decentralized planning and the Panchayat system amount to a reconstitution of Marxism. To be sure, such reconstitution is often camouflaged. It takes the *form* of invoking the authority of Marx (by quoting him) to reconstitute Marxism, but is nonetheless real.

The Marxist methodology of comprehension of reality, in other words, is actually vastly different from what the practitioners claim or may even consciously believe: one does not comprehend reality by seeking 'enlightenment' in Marx's writings; rather, one comprehends reality by reconstituting Marxism and locates the roots of this reconstitution in Marx's writings. Of course, one's comprehension is affected by one's general approach, e.g. historical materialism, which is derived from Marx, but that is at the level of the substructure of the analysis.

In this process, however, certain peaks are reached which stand out above the steady stream of reconstitutions, and carry theoretical comprehension of the historical process up to that moment to a point where, if one may borrow the words of Georg Lukacs, the distinguished Marxist philosopher, 'theory bursts into praxis'.[3] Lenin's work was clearly such a peak. And it is in the context of Lenin's work that Lukacs had said that the highest level of development of theory is when theory 'bursts into praxis', i.e., when it acquires a totality, a width that covers in a unified form, the entire distance from the most general issues of philosophical materialism to the most concrete questions of immediate praxis.

Such a peak in the constitution or reconstitution of Marxist theory, such a level of theoretical comprehension (what was referred to above as 'unified theory') is achieved only episodically, only at certain conjunctures. The *Manifesto* represented such a peak, just as Lenin's work more than half a century later represented another such peak. The *Manifesto*, in other words, is at one level a 'unified theory' of its time; at another level, it provides the core (with flexible boundaries) of all subsequent Marxist theorization.

V

The setbacks which the Communist movement suffered over the last decade had given rise to a euphoric view in bourgeois circles that the days of the Marxist world outlook are over. By now, however, this euphoria has vanished. The condition of the people in Russia and Eastern Europe has gone from bad to worse: if losses in terms of truncated lives are added up, then millions would be found to have died under the free market. The percentage of unemployed workers in Western Europe continues to remain in double digits, and even Japan, the most successful capitalist country of the post-War years, is enmeshed in crisis. In Africa and Latin America stagnation persists: the sharp decline in per capita income of the 1980s may have come to a halt, but it has not been reversed; and further declines are in store in countries like Brazil. In addition, however, there has been a collapse

---

[3] G. Lukacs, *Lenin*, London 1970.

of growth in the developing countries of East and South East Asia. Indeed the entire capitalist world other than the United States and Britain is in the throes of stagnation and high or rising unemployment.

There is a serious possibility of this crisis getting generalized over the entire capitalist world, i.e., becoming a world-wide depression engulfing the U.S. and Britain as well. This possibility arises for the following reason. Periods of high activity in the capitalist world have invariably seen the leading capitalist country of the time running a current account deficit on its balance of payments *vis-a-vis* the other major capitalist countries. In other words, during world capitalist booms the leading capitalist country has provided a market for its rivals within its own boundaries and solved its own market problem by finding additional markets elsewhere, in the colonies or by selling to its own State; and this is what has sustained the boom. The long boom from the mid-nineteenth century to the First World War saw Britain providing a market within its own boundaries to an industrializing Europe, and in turn finding its own market increasingly in China and India. And this is what sustained the long boom. In the post-Second World War years the leading capitalist country, the U.S., ran current account deficits financed by printing dollars (then the reserve currency and decreed 'as good as gold'), while its own markets expanded through large budget deficits. Indeed the essence of the leadership role consists precisely in running such deficits which help the system as a whole to expand. Conversely, depressions are associated with the leader's unwillingness to fulfill this role. Given the fact that the U.S. has of late cut down its fiscal deficit (the reason for this, having to do with the emergence of international finance capital, will be examined later), owing to which its current account deficit in real terms has not expanded in a decade, the conditions for a depression are maturing.

The setback to socialism at this juncture, in the context of the growing disillusionment with capitalism, is responsible for the growth of a whole array of reactionary and fundamentalist tendencies which fill the oppositional space to traditional bourgeois formations. Unemployment in Europe has brought in its train open and vicious racialism. And the response to the pain and humiliation caused over large parts of the Third World by integration with global capitalism has been a fundamentalist one (though not all fundamentalism, especially our own home-grown variety, professes to be anti-imperialist). Such responses are unviable; they have no coherent programme, let alone a programme for emancipation; but they cause much misery to the toiling people.

The real question then is not whether the socialist project would be revitalized, but when. The fact that capitalism is experiencing a profound crisis which may develop into a general depression does not of course automatically entail an immediate revival of socialism. Indeed, if European experience is anything to go by, then the crisis entails a further distancing from socialism of parties which label themselves socialist (the reasons for which we shall explore later). To be sure, this phase of distancing may not last, but the revival of socialism internationally would clearly occur not as an immediate outcome but through a protracted process. Such a process, however, can reach fruition only if there is a re-creation once again of a unified theoretical understanding, of a theory stretching out to praxis, of a reconstituted Marxism scaling new heights. A stylized recounting of certain developments in the contemporary world economy which can form a prelude to such an effort is attempted below.

VI

An important feature of the contemporary world economy is the emergence of international finance capital in a new form. This form differs from what Lenin had written about in at least three ways: first, the Leninist concept referred to finance capital which was essentially nation-based, and consequently nation-state aided. What we see today is finance that constitutes a large international bloc. It gets sucked in from particular countries, and gets deployed in particular areas in search of quick profits without much concern for the nation of its origin. To be sure, there is competition between advanced countries about the location of the financial centre of the capitalist world (of which the development of the Euro is a manifestation), but this competition is not the same as the fragmentation of finance capital into nation-based blocs. Secondly, Lenin's concept referred to 'capital controlled by banks and employed in industry'. This coalescence of finance and industry is of less significance today than pure speculation: the primary form of international finance capital today is 'hot money' flows in search of quick profits. Thirdly, this international finance operates in the context of, and in turn contributes to, a situation of comparative unity (despite contradictions) rather than rivalry among capitalist powers.

Let us examine this last point. Inter-imperialist rivalry jeopardizes the unity of international finance capital, the fact that finance is sucked in from all over to be deployed anywhere. Any such rivalry, which must inevitably manifest itself in some form of discriminatory treatment in one metropolitan country against finance originating in another, runs counter to the current tendency to open up the entire globe for the unfettered operation of international finance capital. The policies of 'liberalization-cum-structural adjustment' being imposed upon the Third World by the Bretton Woods institutions are an expression of this tendency. No doubt, there is not just one motive, but a host of them, underlying the advocacy of these policies, such as the need to prise open Third World markets as a mechanism of 'centralization of capital' on a world scale, especially in a situation of slowdown of growth in the advanced countries, and the need of the advanced countries to obtain tropical primary commodities and other raw materials cheaply. But a very important motive is to prise open the Third World for the operation of international finance capital, which then has the opportunity of making 'killings' through stockmarket booms, and of buying up natural resources, prime land, and public enterprises 'for a song'. This need of finance for unfettered movement across the globe makes its partition into hostile spheres of influence among rival imperialist powers undesirable. And this fact, in turn, acts to keep rivalries in check.

The aftermath of the Second World War had seen a setback for finance capital generally. The triumph of Keynesianism, with its call for the 'euthanasia of the rentier', its advocacy of State intervention, and its prescription of 'cheap money', was an expression of this setback. The process through which finance capital recovered from this setback to acquire ascendancy and a global character need not detain us here. But at least three implications of this ascendancy are important for our discussion.

First, globalized finance capital has undermined the possibility, not only of Keynesian demand management but indeed of any form of significant state intervention. It is not just Keynesianism that is in retreat today but social democracy, welfare capitalism, Third World nationalism, planning in all its different varieties, and all 'isms' that seek to use the state to overcome the problems of spontaneous capitalism. Even the collapse of Soviet-style socialism is not unrelated to the ascendancy of globalized finance: the fact that its contradictions could not be resolved within an altered, but nonetheless socialist, framework was because financial outflows during the last years of Soviet rule, by state-owned enterprises themselves and despite the existence of formal controls, brought the economy to its knees. All reform agendas rely on the state as the agency of intervention, but the state, in order to act effectively, needs a 'control area' over which its writ would run; this 'control area' gets undermined if there is *de facto* (whether or not *de jure*) capital mobility between the country in question and the rest of the world.

Secondly, globalized finance capital is a major cause of crisis and stagnation in world capitalism. Different authors have stressed different factors as underlying the crisis, ranging from a drying up of innovations, to a Kondratieff downswing, to a response to the falling tendency of the rate of profit. Besides, there are important issues relating to the precise delineation and timing of the crisis. But no matter how we demarcate and date the crisis, and no matter what other factors may also underlie it, the fact of globalization of finance has certainly been a contributory factor. It has contributed in at least three ways: first, it has, as mentioned above, made Keynesian policies of demand management difficult in individual countries, because of which governments cannot take counteracting measures; and this accentuates the crisis. Secondly, a world of globalized finance capital is a world with a general tendency towards deflation. We discussed above the fact that inter-imperialist rivalries are kept in check by globalization of finance. Paradoxically, however, competition between countries where each seeks not to have a worse 'investment climate' than the others gets intensified by this globalization. In this competition between countries, deflationary tendencies inevitably thrive: fiscal deficits are generally lowered, and the elimination of inflation comes to acquire prime status among policy objectives, to the detriment of growth. Thirdly, this tendency towards competitive deflation even affects the leading capitalist country without whose active pursuit of expansionary policies and active efforts to transmit such expansion to the rest of the advanced capitalist world (through running current account payments deficits *vis-a-vis* other metropolitan countries), high levels of activity in world capitalism become difficult to sustain. For all these reasons, therefore, the ascendancy of globalized finance contributes to the accentuation and perpetuation, if not the onset, of crisis in the capitalist world.

The third implication of globalized finance is the acute all-round crisis to which it reduces the Third World. It is sometimes argued that since fluidity of finance adversely affects activity levels in all countries, and since the particular national origins of its tributaries become irrelevant for global finance, the globalization of finance makes the concept of imperialism, in the sense of a hiatus between the advanced and backward capitalist worlds, outdated. Nothing could be farther from the truth. The crisis of capitalism that globalized finance becomes associated with afflicts the Third World with particular severity. Just as in any capitalist crisis it is the small capitals that go under, giving rise to centralization of capital, likewise in any global capitalist crisis it is the Third World capitals, and Third World producers in general, which go under, causing centralization on a world scale. And the possibility of any protection is removed because of the *laissez-faire* policies which Bretton Woods institutions (and of late the WTO) championing *inter alia* the interests of globalized finance impose on these economies.

But it is not just in narrow economic terms that the Third World is reduced to a state of crisis. There is a palpable loss of sovereignty as the whims of international financiers (whose 'state of confidence' in the economy acquires paramount importance), rather than the demands of the local population becomes the prime determinant not just of economic policy, but of the entire gamut of policies. This erosion of sovereignty necessitates an attenuation of democracy as well.

The pursuit of policies that boost or retain the 'confidence' of international finance, even when these are contrary to the demands of the people, is possible only if the people's will ceases to matter for the colour of the government, i.e. if democracy is effectively curtailed.

This curtailment occurs in several ways: the first and the most obvious is a scuttling of democracy, or the introduction of institutional 'reforms' that effectively reduce its content, e.g. the call for the 'Presidential form of government' in India, or for fixing ('in the interests of economic development'!) the minimum tenure of the Parliament. Secondly, since bourgeois and social democratic political parties come to adopt similar economic programmes and swear by 'reforms' (a euphemism for the economic agenda of international finance capital), the electorate is often denied any real choice even within the framework of democratic elections. In Argentina, Carlos Menem got elected originally as a Peronist candidate with working class support but implemented anti-working class measures to appease international financiers after coming to power. In Peru Fujimori did the same. In India three successive governments have adopted similar economic policies, the last of them, the BJP-led, in clear contravention of its own pre-election programme. This phenomenon is not simply due to bad faith of certain parties. It is because of the objective constraints of a 'liberalized' economy, where not appeasing international financiers entails economic hardships for the people owing to capital outflows, just as appeasing international financiers does. The problem, in other words, lies in getting into the trap of global finance. Ruling class or social democratic parties which do not have the will to get out of this trap (no doubt by paying the price of transitional difficulties) can scarcely therefore offer an alternative within the confines of a 'liberalized' economy. The choice between them amounts therefore to an attenuation of democracy. Thirdly, a 'liberalized' Third World economy sees the emergence of divisive forces in the form of secessionism, communalism, and ethnic chauvinism, as an accompaniment of stagnation and accentuated unemployment. This produces a 'discourse shift', a political polarization along lines very different from economic programmes.

As the last point suggests, Third World economies caught in the vortex of globalized finance experience a combination of economic crisis, social strife along lines that divide the people, as well as an ero-sion of sovereignty and democracy. It is in this context where the socialist forces offer the only way forward, that the possibility, indeed the inevitability, of a revival of the socialist project in this part of the globe, at any rate, arises. Such a revival would certainly bring about a new unified theory appropriate for its tasks. And the dazzling insights of *The Communist Manifesto* would certainly go into the making of such a new theoretical unity.

Karl Marx and Frederick Engels

Manifesto
of the Communist Party

A spectre is

haunting Europe – the spectre of Communism. All the Powers of old Europe have entered into a holy alliance to exorcise this spectre: Pope and Czar, Metternich and Guizot, French Radicals and German police-spies.

Where is the party in opposition that has not been decried as Communistic by its opponents in power? Where the Opposition that has not hurled back the branding reproach of Communism, against the more advanced opposition parties, as well as against its reactionary adversaries?

Two things result from this fact:

I. Communism is already acknowledged by all European Powers to be itself a Power.

II. It is high time that Communists should openly, in the face of the whole world, publish their views, their aims, their tendencies, and meet this nursery tale of the Spectre of Communism with a Manifesto of the party itself.

To this end, Communists of various nationalities have assembled in London, and sketched the following Manifesto, to be published in the English, French, German, Italian, Flemish and Danish languages.

I Bourgeois and Proletarians*

The history of all hitherto existing society** is the history of class struggles.

Freeman and slave, patrician and plebeian, lord and serf, guild-master*** and journeyman, in a word, oppressor and oppressed, stood in constant opposition to one another, carried on an uninterrupted, now hidden, now open fight, a fight that each time ended, either in a revolutionary re-constitution of society at large, or in the common ruin of the contending classes.

---

* By bourgeoisie is meant the class of modern Capitalists, owners of the means of social production and employers of wage-labour. By proletariat, the class of modern wage-labourers who, having no means of production of their own, are reduced to selling their labour-power in order to live. [Note by Engels to the English edition of 1888.]

** That is, all *written* history. In 1847, the pre-history of society, the social organization existing previous to recorded history, was all but unknown. Since then, Haxthausen discovered common ownership of land in Russia, Maurer proved it to be the social foundation from which all Teutonic races started in history, and by and by village communities were found to be, or to have been the primitive form of society everywhere from India to Ireland. The inner organization of this primitive Communistic society was laid bare, in its typical form, by Morgan's crowning discovery of the true nature of the *gens* and its relation to the *tribe*. With the dissolution of these primeval communities society begins to be differentiated into separate and finally antagonistic classes. I have attempted to retrace this process of dissolution in *Der Ursprung der Familie, des Privateigenthums und des Staats*, second edition, Stuttgart, 1886. [Note by Engels to the English edition of 1888, and – less the last sentence – to the German edition of 1890.]

*** Guild-master, that is, a full member of a guild, a master within, not a head of a guild. [Note by Engels to the English edition of 1888.]

In the earlier epochs of history, we find almost everywhere a complicated arrangement of society into various orders, a manifold gradation of social rank. In ancient Rome we have patricians, knights, plebeians, slaves; in the Middle Ages, feudal lords, vassals, guild-masters, journeymen, apprentices,[1] serfs; in almost all of these classes, again, subordinate gradations.

The modern bourgeois society that has sprouted from the ruins of feudal society has not done away with class antagonisms. It has but established new classes, new conditions of oppression, new forms of struggle in place of the old ones.

Our epoch, the epoch of the bourgeoisie, possesses, however, this distinctive feature: it has simplified the class antagonisms. Society as a whole is more and more splitting up into two great hostile camps, into two great classes directly facing each other: Bourgeoisie and Proletariat.

From the serfs of the Middle Ages sprang the chartered burghers of the earliest towns. From these burgesses the first elements of the bourgeoisie were developed.

The discovery of America, the rounding of the Cape, opened up fresh ground for the rising bourgeoisie. The East-Indian and Chinese markets, the colonization of America, trade with the colonies, the increase in the means of exchange and in commodities generally, gave to commerce, to navigation, to industry, an impulse never before known, and thereby, to the revolutionary element in the tottering feudal society, a rapid development.

The feudal system of industry, under which industrial production was monopolized by closed guilds,[2] now no longer sufficed for the growing wants of the new markets. The manufacturing system took its place. The guild-masters were pushed on one side by the manufacturing middle class;[3] division of labour between the

---

[1] The German editions of 1848, 1872, 1883 and 1890 have 'journeymen' ('Gesellen') instead of 'journeymen, apprentices'.

[2] In the German editions the beginning of the phrase is: 'The former feudal, or guild, organization of industry'.

[3] The German editions have here and below 'middle estate' ('Mittelstand') instead of 'middle class'.

different corporate guilds vanished in the face of division of labour in each single workshop.

Meantime the markets kept ever growing, the demand ever rising. Even manufacture no longer sufficed. Thereupon, steam and machinery revolutionized industrial production. The place of manufacture was taken by the giant, Modern Industry, the place of the industrial middle class, by industrial millionaires, the leaders of whole industrial armies, the modern bourgeois.

Modern[4] industry has established the world market, for which the discovery of America paved the way. This market has given an immense development to commerce, to navigation, to communication by land. This development has, in its turn, reacted on the extension of industry; and in proportion as industry, commerce, navigation, railways extended, in the same proportion the bourgeoisie developed, increased its capital, and pushed into the background every class handed down from the Middle Ages.

We see, therefore, how the modern bourgeoisie is itself the product of a long course of development, of a series of revolutions in the modes of production and of exchange.

Each step in the development of the bourgeoisie was accompanied by a corresponding political advance of that class.[5] An oppressed class[6] under the sway of the feudal nobility, an armed and self-governing association in the medieval commune;* here independent urban republic (as in Italy and Germany), there taxable 'third estate' of

---

* 'Commune' was the name taken, in France, by the nascent towns even before they had conquered from their feudal lords and masters local self-government and political rights as the 'Third Estate'. Generally speaking, for the economical development of the bourgeoisie, England is here taken as the typical country; for its political development, France. [Note by Engels to the English edition of 1888.]

    This was the name given their urban communities by the townsmen of Italy and France, after they had purchased or wrested their initial rights of self-government from their feudal lords. [Note by Engels to the German edition of 1890.]

---

[4] The German editions have here and below 'large-scale' instead of 'modern'.

[5] The words 'of that class' were added in the English edition of 1888.

[6] The German editions have 'estate' instead of 'class'.

the monarchy (as in France),[7] afterwards, in the period of manufacture proper, serving either the semi-feudal[8] or the absolute monarchy as a counterpoise against the nobility, and, in fact, cornerstone of the great monarchies in general, the bourgeoisie has at last, since the establishment of Modern Industry and of the world market, conquered for itself, in the modern representative State, exclusive political sway. The executive of the modern State is but a committee for managing the common affairs of the whole bourgeoisie.

The bourgeoisie, historically, has played a most revolutionary part.

The bourgeoisie, wherever it has got the upper hand, has put an end to all feudal, patriarchal, idyllic relations. It has pitilessly torn asunder the motley feudal ties that bound man to his 'natural superiors', and has left remaining no other nexus between man and man than naked self-interest, than callous 'cash payment'. It has drowned the most heavenly ecstasies of religious fervour, of chivalrous enthusiasm, of philistine sentimentalism, in the icy water of egotistical calculation. It has resolved personal worth into exchange value, and in place of the numberless indefeasible chartered freedoms, has set up that single, unconscionable freedom – Free Trade. In one word, for exploitation, veiled by religious and political illusions, it has substituted naked, shameless, direct, brutal exploitation.

The bourgeoisie has stripped of its halo every occupation hitherto honoured and looked up to with reverent awe. It has converted the physician, the lawyer, the priest, the poet, the man of science, into its paid wage-labourers.

The bourgeoisie has torn away from the family its sentimental veil, and has reduced the family relation to a mere money relation.

The bourgeoisie has disclosed how it came to pass that the brutal display of vigour in the Middle Ages, which Reactionists so much admire, found its fitting complement in the most slothful indolence. It has been the first to show what man's activity can bring about. It has accomplished wonders far surpassing Egyptian pyramids, Roman

---

[7] The words 'medieval', '(as in Italy and Germany)', '(as in France)'were added in the English edition of 1888.
[8] The German editions have 'estate' instead of 'semi-feudal'.

aqueducts, and Gothic cathedrals; it has conducted expeditions that put in the shade all former Exoduses of nations and crusades.

The bourgeoisie cannot exist without constantly revolutionizing the instruments of production, and thereby the relations of production, and with them the whole relations of society. Conservation of the old modes of production in unaltered form, was, on the contrary, the first condition of existence for all earlier industrial classes. Constant revolutionizing of production, uninterrupted disturbance of all social conditions, everlasting uncertainty and agitation distinguish the bourgeois epoch from all earlier ones. All fixed, fast-frozen relations, with their train of ancient and venerable prejudices and opinions, are swept away, all new-formed ones become antiquated before they can ossify. All that is solid melts into air, all that is holy is profaned, and man is at last compelled to face with sober senses, his real conditions of life, and his relations with his kind.

The need of a constantly expanding market for its products chases the bourgeoisie over the whole surface of the globe. It must nestle everywhere, settle everywhere, establish connections everywhere.

The bourgeoisie has through its exploitation of the world market given a cosmopolitan character to production and consumption in every country. To the great chagrin of Reactionists, it has drawn from under the feet of industry the national ground on which it stood. All old-established national industries have been destroyed or are daily being destroyed. They are dislodged by new industries, whose introduction becomes a life and death question for all civilized nations, by industries that no longer work up indigenous raw material, but raw material drawn from the remotest zones; industries whose products are consumed, not only at home, but in every quarter of the globe. In place of the old wants, satisfied by the productions of the country, we find new wants, requiring for their satisfaction the products of distant lands and climes. In place of the old local and national seclusion and self-sufficiency, we have intercourse in every direction, universal inter-dependence of nations. And as in material, so also in intellectual production. The intellectual creations of individual nations become common property. National one-sidedness and narrow-mindedness become more and more impossible, and from the numerous national and local literatures, there arises a world literature.

The bourgeoisie, by the rapid improvement of all instruments of production, by the immensely facilitated means of communication, draws all, even the most barbarian, nations into civilization. The cheap prices of its commodities are the heavy artillery with which it batters down all Chinese walls, with which it forces the barbarians' intensely obstinate hatred of foreigners to capitulate. It compels all nations, on pain of extinction, to adopt the bourgeois mode of production; it compels them to introduce what it calls civilization into their midst, i.e., to become bourgeois themselves. In one word, it creates a world after its own image.

The bourgeoisie has subjected the country to the rule of the towns. It has created enormous cities, has greatly increased the urban population as compared with the rural, and has thus rescued a considerable part of the population from the idiocy of rural life. Just as it has made the country dependent on the towns, so it has made barbarian and semi-barbarian countries dependent on the civilized ones, nations of peasants on nations of bourgeois, the East on the West.

The bourgeoisie keeps more and more doing away with the scattered state of the population, of the means of production, and of property. It has agglomerated population, centralized means of production, and has concentrated property in a few hands. The necessary consequence of this was political centralization. Independent, or but loosely connected provinces with separate interests, laws, governments and systems of taxation, became lumped together into one nation, with one government, one code of laws, one national class-interest, one frontier and one customs-tariff.

The bourgeoisie, during its rule of scarce one hundred years, has created more massive and more colossal productive forces than have all preceding generations together. Subjection of Nature's forces to man, machinery, application of chemistry to industry and agriculture, steam-navigation, railways, electric telegraphs, clearing of whole continents for cultivation, canalization of rivers, whole populations conjured out of the ground – what earlier century had even a presentiment that such productive forces slumbered in the lap of social labour?

We see then: the means of production and of exchange, on whose foundation the bourgeoisie built itself up, were generated in feudal society. At a certain stage in the development of these means of production and of exchange, the conditions under which feudal society produced and exchanged, the feudal organization of agriculture and manufacturing industry, in one word, the feudal relations of property became no longer compatible with the already developed productive forces;[9] they became so many fetters. They had to be burst asunder; they were burst asunder.

Into their place stepped free competition, accompanied by a social and political constitution adapted to it, and by the economical and political sway of the bourgeois class.

A similar movement is going on before our own eyes. Modern bourgeois society with its relations of production, of exchange and of property, a society that has conjured up such gigantic means of production and of exchange, is like the sorcerer, who is no longer able to control the powers of the nether world whom he has called up by his spells. For many a decade past the history of industry and commerce is but the history of the revolt of modern productive forces against modern conditions of production, against the property relations that are the conditions for the existence of the bourgeoisie and of its rule. It is enough to mention the commercial crises that by their periodical return put on its trial, each time more threateningly, the existence of the entire bourgeois society. In these crises a great part not only of the existing products, but also of the previously created productive forces, are periodically destroyed. In these crises there breaks out an epidemic[10] that, in all earlier epochs, would have seemed an absurdity – the epidemic of over-production. Society suddenly finds itself put back into a state of momentary barbarism; it appears as if a famine, a universal war of devastation had cut off the supply of every means of subsistence; industry and commerce seem to be destroyed; and why? Because there is too much civilization, too much means of subsistence, too much industry, too much commerce. The productive forces at the disposal of society no longer tend to further the development of the conditions of bourgeois property;[11] on the contrary, they have

---

[9] The German editions add: 'they hindered production instead of developing it'.

[10] The German editions have: 'a social epidemic'.

[11] The German editions of 1848 have: 'bourgeois civilization and the conditions of bourgeois property'.

become too powerful for these conditions, by which they are fettered, and so soon as they overcome these fetters, they bring disorder into the whole of bourgeois society, endanger the existence of bourgeois property. The conditions of bourgeois society are too narrow to comprise the wealth created by them. And how does the bourgeoisie get over these crises? On the one hand by enforced destruction of a mass of productive forces; on the other, by the conquest of new markets, and by the more thorough exploitation of the old ones. That is to say, by paving the way for more extensive and more destructive crises, and by diminishing the means whereby crises are prevented.

The weapons with which the bourgeoisie felled feudalism to the ground are now turned against the bourgeoisie itself.

But not only has the bourgeoisie forged the weapons that bring death to itself; it has also called into existence the men who are to wield those weapons – the modern working class – the proletarians.[12]

In proportion as the bourgeoisie, i.e., capital, is developed, in the same proportion is the proletariat, the modern working class, developed – a class of labourers, who live only so long as they find work, and who find work only so long as their labour increases capital. These labourers, who must sell themselves piecemeal, are a commodity, like every other article of commerce, and are consequently exposed to all the vicissitudes of competition, to all the fluctuations of the market.

Owing to the extensive use of machinery and to division of labour, the work of the proletarians has lost all individual character, and, consequently, all charm for the workman. He becomes an appendage of the machine, and it is only the most simple, most monotonous, and most easily acquired knack, that is required of him. Hence, the cost of production of a workman is restricted, almost entirely, to the means of subsistence that he requires for his maintenance, and for the propagation of his race. But the price of a commodity, and therefore also of labour, is equal to its cost of production. In proportion, therefore, as the repulsiveness of the work increases, the wage decreases. Nay more, in proportion as the use of machinery and division of labour increases, in the same proportion the burden of toil[13] also increases, whether by

---

12 The German editions have: 'the modern workers, the *proletarians*'.
13 The German editions have: 'the quantity of labour'.

prolongation of the working hours, by increase of the work exacted in a given time or by increased speed of the machinery, etc.

Modern industry has converted the little workshop of the patriarchal master into the great factory of the industrial capitalist. Masses of labourers, crowded into the factory, are organized like soldiers. As privates of the industrial army they are placed under the command of a perfect hierarchy of officers and sergeants. Not only are they slaves of the bourgeois class, and of the bourgeois State; they are daily and hourly enslaved by the machine, by the overlooker, and, above all, by the individual bourgeois manufacturer himself. The more openly this despotism proclaims gain to be its end and aim, the more petty, the more hateful and the more embittering it is.

The less the skill and exertion of strength implied in manual labour, in other words, the more modern industry becomes developed, the more is the labour of men superseded by that of women.[14] Differences of age and sex have no longer any distinctive social validity for the working class. All are instruments of labour, more or less expensive to use, according to their age and sex.

No sooner is the exploitation of the labourer by the manufacturer, so far, at an end, and he receives his wages in cash, than he is set upon by the other portions of the bourgeoisie, the landlord, the shopkeeper, the pawnbroker, etc.

The lower strata of the middle class[15] – the small tradespeople, shopkeepers, and retired tradesmen generally,[16] the handicraftsmen and peasants – all these sink gradually into the proletariat, partly because their diminutive capital does not suffice for the scale on which Modern Industry is carried on, and is swamped in the competition with the large capitalists, partly because their specialized skill is rendered worthless by new methods of production. Thus the proletariat is recruited from all classes of the population.

The proletariat goes through various stages of development. With its birth begins its struggle with the bourgeoisie. At first the contest is carried on by individual labourers, then by the workpeople of a

---

[14] The German 23-page edition of 1848 has: 'of women and children'.

[15] The German editions have: 'The former lower strata of the middle estate'.

[16] The German editions have: 'and rentiers' instead of 'and retired tradesmen generally'.

factory, then by the operatives of one trade, in one locality, against the individual bourgeois who directly exploits them. They direct their attacks not against the bourgeois conditions of production, but against the instruments of production themselves;[17] they destroy imported wares that compete with their labour, they smash to pieces machinery, they set factories ablaze, they seek to restore by force the vanished status of the workman of the Middle Ages.

At this stage the labourers still form an incoherent[18] mass scattered over the whole country, and broken up by their mutual competition. If anywhere they unite to form more compact bodies, this is not yet the consequence of their own active union, but of the union of the bourgeoisie, which class, in order to attain its own political ends, is compelled to set the whole proletariat in motion, and is moreover yet, for a time, able to do so. At this stage, therefore, the proletarians do not fight their enemies, but the enemies of their enemies, the remnants of absolute monarchy, the landowners, the non-industrial bourgeois, the petty bourgeoisie. Thus the whole historical movement is concentrated in the hands of the bourgeoisie; every victory so obtained is a victory for the bourgeoisie.

But with the development of industry the proletariat not only increases in number; it becomes concentrated in greater masses, its strength grows, and it feels that strength more. The various interests and conditions of life within the ranks of the proletariat are more and more equalized, in proportion as machinery obliterates all distinctions of labour, and nearly everywhere reduces wages to the same low level. The growing competition among the bourgeois, and the resulting commercial crises, make the wages of the workers ever more fluctuating. The unceasing improvement of machinery, ever more rapidly developing, makes their livelihood more and more precarious; the collisions between individual workmen and individual bourgeois take more and more the character of collisions between two classes. Thereupon the workers begin to form combinations (Trades' Unions)[19]

---

[17] The German editions have: 'They direct their attacks not only against the bourgeois conditions of production, they direct them against the instruments of production themselves'.

[18] This word was inserted in the English edition of 1888.

[19] The words in parentheses were inserted in the English edition of 1888.

against the bourgeois; they club together in order to keep up the rate of wages; they found permanent associations in order to make provision beforehand for these occasional revolts. Here and there the contest breaks out into riots.

Now and then the workers are victorious, but only for a time. The real fruit of their battles lies, not in the immediate result, but in the ever-expanding union of the workers. This union is helped on by the improved means of communication that are created by modern industry and that place the workers of different localities in contact with one another. It was just this contact that was needed to centralize the numerous local struggles, all of the same character, into one national struggle between classes. But every class struggle is a political struggle. And that union, to attain which the burghers of the Middle Ages, with their miserable highways, required centuries, the modern proletarians, thanks to railways, achieve in a few years.

This organization of the proletarians into a class, and consequently into a political party, is continually being upset again by the competition between the workers themselves. But it ever rises up again, stronger, firmer, mightier. It compels legislative recognition of particular interests of the workers, by taking advantage of the divisions among the bourgeoisie itself. Thus the ten-hours' bill in England was carried.

Altogether collisions between the classes of the old society further, in many ways, the course of development of the proletariat. The bourgeoisie finds itself involved in a constant battle. At first with the aristocracy; later on, with those portions of the bourgeoisie itself, whose interests have become antagonistic to the progress of industry; at all times, with the bourgeoisie of foreign countries. In all these battles it sees itself compelled to appeal to the proletariat, to ask for its help, and thus, to drag it into the political arena. The bourgeoisie itself, therefore, supplies the proletariat with its own elements of political and general[20] education, in other words, it furnishes the proletariat with weapons for fighting the bourgeoisie.

Further, as we have already seen, entire sections of the ruling classes are, by the advance of industry, precipitated into the

---

[20] The words 'political and general' were added in the English edition of 1888.

proletariat, or are at least threatened in their conditions of existence. These also supply the proletariat with fresh elements of enlightenment and progress.[21]

Finally, in times when the class struggle nears the decisive hour, the process of dissolution going on within the ruling class, in fact within the whole range of old society, assumes such a violent, glaring character, that a small section of the ruling class cuts itself adrift, and joins the revolutionary class, the class that holds the future in its hands. Just as, therefore, at an earlier period, a section of the nobility went over to the bourgeoisie, so now a portion of the bourgeoisie goes over to the proletariat, and in particular, a portion of the bourgeois ideologists, who have raised themselves to the level of comprehending theoretically the historical movement as a whole.

Of all the classes that stand face to face with the bourgeoisie today, the proletariat alone is a really revolutionary class. The other classes decay and finally disappear in the face of Modern Industry; the proletariat is its special and essential product.

The lower middle class,[22] the small manufacturer, the shopkeeper, the artisan, the peasant, all these fight against the bourgeoisie, to save from extinction their existence as fractions of the middle class. They are therefore not revolutionary, but conservative. Nay more, they are reactionary, for they try to roll back the wheel of history. If by chance they are revolutionary, they are so only in view of their impending transfer into the proletariat, they thus defend not their present, but their future interests, they desert their own standpoint to place themselves at that of the proletariat.

The 'dangerous class', the social scum,[23] that passively rotting mass thrown off by the lowest layers of old society may, here and there, be swept into the movement by a proletarian revolution; its conditions of life, however, prepare it far more for the part of a bribed tool of reactionary intrigue.

---

21 The German editions have 'elements of education' instead of 'elements of enlightenment and progress'.

22 The German editions have here and below 'middle estates' instead of 'the lower middle class' and 'the middle class'.

23 The German editions have 'lumpen proletariat' instead of 'the dangerous class, the social scum'.

In the conditions of the proletariat, those of old society at large are already virtually swamped. The proletarian is without property; his relation to his wife and children has no longer anything in common with the bourgeois family relations; modern industrial labour, modern subjection to capital, the same in England as in France, in America as in Germany, has stripped him of every trace of national character. Law, morality, religion, are to him so many bourgeois prejudices, behind which lurk in ambush just as many bourgeois interests.

All the preceding classes that got the upper hand, sought to fortify their already acquired status by subjecting society at large to their conditions of appropriation. The proletarians cannot become masters of the productive forces of society, except by abolishing their own previous mode of appropriation, and thereby also every other previous mode of appropriation. They have nothing of their own to secure and to fortify; their mission is to destroy all previous securities for, and insurances of, individual property.

All previous historical[24] movements were movements of minorities, or in the interest of minorities. The proletarian movement is the self-conscious,[25] independent movement of the immense majority, in the interest of the immense majority. The proletariat, the lowest stratum of our present society, cannot stir, cannot raise itself up, without the whole superincumbent strata of official society being sprung into the air.

Though not in substance, yet in form, the struggle of the proletariat with the bourgeoisie is at first a national struggle. The proletariat of each country must, of course, first of all settle matters with its own bourgeoisie.

In depicting the most general phases of the development of the proletariat, we traced the more or less veiled civil war, raging within existing society, up to the point where that war breaks out into open revolution, and where the violent overthrow of the bourgeoisie lays the foundation for the sway of the proletariat.

Hitherto, every form of society has been based, as we have already seen, on the antagonism of oppressing and oppressed classes.

---

[24] This word was added in the English edition of 1888.
[25] This word was added in the English edition of 1888.

But in order to oppress a class, certain conditions must be assured to it under which it can, at least, continue its slavish existence. The serf, in the period of serfdom, raised himself to membership in the commune, just as the petty bourgeois, under the yoke of feudal absolutism, managed to develop into a bourgeois. The modern labourer, on the contrary, instead of rising with the progress of industry, sinks deeper and deeper below the conditions of existence of his own class. He becomes a pauper, and pauperism develops more rapidly than population and wealth. And here it becomes evident, that the bourgeoisie is unfit any longer to be the ruling class in society, and to impose its conditions of existence upon society as an over-riding law. It is unfit to rule because it is incompetent to assure an existence to its slave within his slavery, because it cannot help letting him sink into such a state, that it has to feed him, instead of being fed by him. Society can no longer live under this bourgeoisie, in other words, its existence is no longer compatible with society.

The essential condition for the existence, and for the sway of the bourgeois class, is[26] the formation and augmentation of capital; the condition for capital is wage-labour. Wage-labour rests exclusively on competition between the labourers. The advance of industry, whose involuntary promoter is the bourgeoisie, replaces the isolation of the labourers, due to competition, by their revolutionary combination, due to association. The development of Modern Industry, therefore, cuts from under its feet the very foundation on which the bourgeoisie produces and appropriates products. What the bourgeoisie, therefore, produces, above all, is its own grave-diggers. Its fall and the victory of the proletariat are equally inevitable.

II Proletarians and Communists

In what relation do the Communists stand to the proletarians as a whole?

The Communists do not form a separate party opposed to other working-class parties.

---

[26] The German editions have here: 'the accumulation of wealth in the hands of individuals'.

They have no interests separate and apart from those of the proletariat as a whole.

They do not set up any sectarian[27] principles of their own, by which to shape and mould the proletarian movement.

The Communists are distinguished from the other working-class parties by this only: 1. In the national struggles of the proletarians of the different countries, they point out and bring to the front the common interests of the entire proletariat, independently of all nationality. 2. In the various stages of development which the struggle of the working class against the bourgeoisie has to pass through, they always and everywhere represent the interests of the movement as a whole.

The Communists, therefore, are on the one hand, practically, the most advanced and[28] resolute section of the working-class parties of every country, that section which pushes forward all others; on the other hand, theoretically, they have over the great mass of the proletariat the advantage of clearly understanding the line of march, the conditions, and the ultimate general results of the proletarian movement.

The immediate aim of the Communists is the same as that of all the other proletarian parties: formation of the proletariat into a class, overthrow of the bourgeois supremacy, conquest of political power by the proletariat.

The theoretical conclusions of the Communists are in no way based on ideas or principles that have been invented, or discovered by this or that would-be universal reformer.

They merely express, in general terms, actual relations springing from an existing class struggle, from a historical movement going on under our very eyes. The abolition of existing property relations is not at all a distinctive feature of Communism.

All property relations in the past have continually been subject to historical change consequent upon the change in historical conditions.[29]

---

[27] The German editions have 'separate' instead of 'sectarian'.
[28] The words 'the most advanced and' were added in the English edition of 1888.
[29] In the German editions this phrase reads: 'All property relations have been subject to constant historical replacement, constant historical change'.

The French Revolution, for example, abolished feudal property in favour of bourgeois property.

The distinguishing feature of Communism is not the abolition of property generally, but the abolition of bourgeois property. But modern bourgeois private property is the final and most complete expression of the system of producing and appropriating products, that is based on class antagonisms, on the exploitation of the many by the few.[30]

In this sense, the theory of the Communists may be summed up in the single sentence: Abolition of private property.

We Communists have been reproached with the desire of abolishing the right of personally acquiring property as the fruit of a man's own labour, which property is alleged to be the groundwork of all personal freedom, activity and independence.

Hard-won, self-acquired, self-earned property! Do you mean the property of the petty artisan[31] and of the small peasant, a form of property that preceded the bourgeois form? There is no need to abolish that; the development of industry has to a great extent already destroyed it, and is still destroying it daily.

Or do you mean modern bourgeois private property?

But does wage-labour create any property for the labourer? Not a bit. It creates capital, i.e., that kind of property which exploits wage-labour, and which cannot increase except upon condition of begetting a new supply of wage-labour for fresh exploitation. Property, in its present form, is based on the antagonism of capital and wage-labour. Let us examine both sides of this antagonism.

To be a capitalist is to have not only a purely personal, but a social status in production. Capital is a collective product, and only by the united action of many members, nay, in the last resort, only by the united action of all members of society, can it be set in motion.

Capital is, therefore, not a personal, it is a social power.

When, therefore, capital is converted into common property, into the property of all members of society, personal property is not thereby

---

[30] The German editions have: 'the exploitation of the ones by the others'.
[31] The German editions have: 'the property of the petty bourgeois'.

transformed into social property. It is only the social character of the property that is changed. It loses its class character.

Let us now take wage-labour.

The average price of wage-labour is the minimum wage, i.e., that quantum of the means of subsistence, which is absolutely requisite to keep the labourer in bare existence as a labourer. What, therefore, the wage-labourer appropriates by means of his labour, merely suffices to prolong and reproduce a bare existence. We by no means intend to abolish this personal appropriation of the products of labour, an appropriation that is made for the maintenance and reproduction of human life, and that leaves no surplus wherewith to command the labour of others. All that we want to do away with is the miserable character of this appropriation, under which the labourer lives merely to increase capital, and is allowed to live only in so far as the interest of the ruling class requires it.

In bourgeois society, living labour is but a means to increase accumulated labour. In Communist society, accumulated labour is but a means to widen, to enrich, to promote the existence of the labourer.

In bourgeois society, therefore, the past dominates the present; in Communist society, the present dominates the past. In bourgeois society capital is independent and has individuality, while the living person is dependent and has no individuality.

And the abolition of this state of things is called by the bourgeois abolition of individuality and freedom! And rightly so. The abolition of bourgeois individuality, bourgeois independence, and bourgeois freedom is undoubtedly aimed at.

By freedom is meant, under the present bourgeois conditions of production, free trade, free selling and buying.

But if selling and buying disappears, free selling and buying disappears also. This talk about free selling and buying, and all the other 'brave words' of our bourgeoisie about freedom in general, have a meaning, if any, only in contrast with restricted selling and buying, with the fettered traders of the Middle Ages, but have no meaning when opposed to the Communistic abolition of buying and selling, of the bourgeois conditions of production, and of the bourgeoisie itself.

You are horrified at our intending to do away with private

property. But in your existing society, private property is already done away with for nine-tenths of the population; its existence for the few[32] is solely due to its non-existence in the hands of those nine-tenths. You reproach us, therefore, with intending to do away with a form of property, the necessary condition for whose existence is the non-existence of any property for the immense majority of society.

In one word, you reproach us with intending to do away with your property. Precisely so; that is just what we intend.

From the moment when labour can no longer be converted into capital, money, or rent, into a social power capable of being monopolized, i.e., from the moment when individual property can no longer be transformed into bourgeois property, into capital,[33] from that moment, you say, individuality vanishes.

You must, therefore, confess that by 'individual' you mean no other person than the bourgeois, than the middle-class owner of property. This person must, indeed, be swept out of the way, and made impossible.[34]

Communism deprives no man of the power to appropriate the products of society; all that it does is to deprive him of the power to subjugate the labour of others by means of such appropriation.

It has been objected that upon the abolition of private property all work will cease, and universal laziness will overtake us.

According to this, bourgeois society ought long ago to have gone to the dogs through sheer idleness; for those of its members who work, acquire nothing, and those who acquire anything, do not work. The whole of this objection is but another expression of the tautology: that there can no longer be any wage-labour when there is no longer any capital.

All objections urged against the Communistic mode of producing and appropriating material products, have, in the same way, been urged against the Communistic modes of producing and appropriating intellectual products. Just as, to the bourgeois, the disappearance of class property is the disappearance of production itself, so the

---

[32] The words 'for the few' were added in the English edition of 1888.
[33] The words 'into capital' were added in the English edition of 1888.
[34] The words 'and made impossible' were added in the English edition of 1888.

disappearance of class culture[35] is to him identical with the disappearance of all culture.

That culture, the loss of which he laments, is, for the enormous majority, a mere training to act as a machine.

But don't wrangle with us so long as you apply, to our intended[36] abolition of bourgeois property, the standard of your bourgeois notions of freedom, culture, law, &c. Your very ideas are but the outgrowth of the conditions of your bourgeois production and bourgeois property, just as your jurisprudence is but the will of your class made into a law for all, a will, whose essential character and direction are determined by the economical conditions of existence of your class.[37]

The selfish misconception that induces you to transform into eternal laws of nature and of reason, the social forms springing from your present mode of production and form of property – historical relations that rise and disappear in the progress of production – this misconception you share with every ruling class that has preceded you.[38] What you see clearly in the case of ancient property, what you admit in the case of feudal property, you are of course forbidden to admit in the case of your own bourgeois form of property.

Abolition of the family! Even the most radical flare up at this infamous proposal of the Communists.

On what foundation is the present family, the bourgeois family, based? On capital, on private gain. In its completely developed form this family exists only among the bourgeoisie. But this state of things finds its complement in the practical absence of the family among the proletarians, and in public prostitution.

The bourgeois family will vanish as a matter of course when its complement vanishes, and both will vanish with the vanishing of capital.

---

[35] The German editions have here and below 'education' ['Bildung'] instead of 'culture'.

[36] The words 'our intended' were inserted in the English edition of 1888.

[37] In the German editions the end of this sentence reads as follows: 'a will, whose content is determined by the material conditions of existence of your class'.

[38] In the German editions this sentence reads as follows: 'This selfish conception... you share with all the ruling classes which have perished'.

Do you charge us with wanting to stop the exploitation of children by their parents? To this crime we plead guilty.

But, you will say, we destroy the most hallowed of relations, when we replace home education by social.

And your education! Is not that also social, and determined by the social conditions under which you educate, by the intervention, direct or indirect, of society, by means of schools, &c.? The Communists have not invented the intervention of society in education; they do but seek to alter the character of that intervention, and to rescue education from the influence of the ruling class.

The bourgeois clap-trap about the family and education, about the hallowed co-relation of parent and child, becomes all the more disgusting, the more, by the action of Modern Industry, all family ties among the proletarians are torn asunder, and their children transformed into simple articles of commerce and instruments of labour.

But you Communists would introduce community of women, screams the whole bourgeoisie in chorus.

The bourgeois sees in his wife a mere instrument of production. He hears that the instruments of production are to be exploited in common, and, naturally, can come to no other conclusion than that the lot of being common to all will likewise fall to the women.

He has not even a suspicion that the real point aimed at is to do away with the status of women as mere instruments of production.

For the rest, nothing is more ridiculous than the virtuous indignation of our bourgeois at the community of women which, they pretend, is to be openly and officially established by the Communists. The Communists have no need to introduce community of women; it has existed almost from time immemorial.

Our bourgeois, not content with having the wives and daughters of their proletarians at their disposal, not to speak of common prostitutes, take the greatest pleasure in seducing each other's wives.

Bourgeois marriage is in reality a system of wives in common and thus, at the most, what the Communists might possibly be reproached with, is that they desire to introduce, in substitution for a hypocritically concealed, an openly legalized community of women. For the rest, it is self-evident that the abolition of the present system of production must bring with it the abolition of the community of women springing from that system, i.e., of prostitution both public and private.

The Communists are further reproached with desiring to abolish countries and nationality.

The working men have no country. We cannot take from them what they have not got. Since the proletariat must first of all acquire political supremacy, must rise to be the leading class of the nation,[39] must constitute itself *the* nation, it is so far, itself national, though not in the bourgeois sense of the word.

National differences and antagonisms between peoples are daily more and more vanishing, owing to the development of the bourgeoisie, to freedom of commerce, to the world market, to uniformity in the mode of production and in the conditions of life corresponding thereto.

The supremacy of the proletariat will cause them to vanish still faster. United action, of the leading civilized countries at least, is one of the first conditions for the emancipation of the proletariat.

In proportion as the exploitation of one individual by another is put an end to, the exploitation of one nation by another will also be put an end to. In proportion as the antagonism between classes within the nation vanishes, the hostility of one nation to another will come to an end.

The charges against Communism made from a religious, a philosophical, and, generally, from an ideological standpoint, are not deserving of serious examination.

Does it require deep intuition to comprehend that man's ideas, views and conceptions, in one word, man's consciousness, changes with every change in the conditions of his material[40] existence, in his social relations and in his social life?

What else does the history of ideas prove, than that intellectual production changes its character in proportion as material production is changed? The ruling ideas of each age have ever been the ideas of its ruling class.

---

[39] The German editions of 1848 have 'the national class' instead of 'the leading class of the nation'.

[40] The word 'material' was added in the English edition of 1888.

When people speak of ideas that revolutionize society, they do but express the fact, that within the old society, the elements of a new one have been created, and that the dissolution of the old ideas keeps even pace with the dissolution of the old conditions of existence.

When the ancient world was in its last throes, the ancient religions were overcome by Christianity. When Christian ideas succumbed in the eighteenth century to rationalist ideas,[41] feudal society fought its death battle with the then revolutionary bourgeoisie. The ideas of religious liberty and freedom of conscience merely gave expression to the sway of free competition within the domain of knowledge.

'Undoubtedly,' it will be said, 'religious, moral, philosophical and juridical ideas[42] have been modified in the course of historical development. But religion, morality, philosophy, political science, and law, constantly survived this change.

'There are, besides, eternal truths, such as Freedom, Justice, etc., that are common to all states of society. But Communism abolishes eternal truths, it abolishes all religion and all morality, instead of constituting them on a new basis; it therefore acts in contradiction to all past historical experience'.

What does this accusation reduce itself to? The history of all past society has consisted in the development of class antagonisms, antagonisms that assumed different forms at different epochs.

But whatever form they may have taken, one fact is common to all past ages, viz., the exploitation of one part of society by the other. No wonder, then, that the social consciousness of past ages, despite all the multiplicity and variety it displays, moves within certain common forms, or general ideas,[43] which cannot completely vanish except with the total disappearance of class antagonisms.

The Communist revolution is the most radical rupture with

---

[41] The German editions have 'the ideas of enlightenment' instead of 'rationalist ideas'.

[42] In the German editions the beginning of the sentence reads: "'Undoubtedly,' it will be said, "religious, moral, philosophical, political, juridical ideas, etc."'

[43] The German editions have 'in forms of consciousness' instead of 'or general ideas'.

traditional property relations; no wonder that its development involves the most radical rupture with traditional ideas.

But let us have done with the bourgeois objections to Communism.

We have seen above, that the first step in the revolution by the working class is to raise the proletariat to the position of ruling class, to win the battle of democracy.

The proletariat will use its political supremacy to wrest, by degrees, all capital from the bourgeoisie, to centralize all instruments of production in the hands of the State, i.e., of the proletariat organized as the ruling class; and to increase the total of productive forces as rapidly as possible.

Of course, in the beginning, this cannot be effected except by means of despotic inroads on the rights of property, and on the conditions of bourgeois production; by means of measures, therefore, which appear economically insufficient and untenable, but which, in the course of the movement, outstrip themselves, necessitate further inroads upon the old social order,[44] and are unavoidable as a means of entirely revolutionizing the mode of production.

The measures will of course be different in different countries.

Nevertheless in the most advanced countries, the following will be pretty generally applicable:

1. Abolition[45] of property in land and application of all rents of land to public purposes.

2. A heavy progressive or graduated income tax.[46]

3. Abolition of all right of inheritance.

4. Confiscation of the property of all emigrants and rebels.

5. Centralization of credit in the hands of the State, by means of a national bank with State capital and an exclusive monopoly.

6. Centralization of the means of communication and transport[47] in the hands of the State.

---

[44] The words 'necessitate further inroads upon the old social order' were added in the English edition of 1888.

[45] The German editions have here 'expropriation'.

[46] The German editions have: 'A heavy progressive tax.'

[47] The German editions have 'all transport' instead of 'the means of communication and transport'.

7. Extension of factories and instruments of production owned by the State; the bringing into cultivation of waste-lands, and the improvement of the soil generally in accordance with a common plan.

8. Equal liability of all to labour. Establishment of industrial armies, especially for agriculture.

9. Combination of agriculture with manufacturing industries; gradual abolition of the distinction between town and country, by a more equable distribution of the population over the country.[48]

10. Free education for all children in public schools. Abolition of children's factory labour in its present form. Combination of education with industrial production, &c., &c.

When, in the course of development, class distinctions have disappeared, and all production has been concentrated in the hands of a vast association of the whole nation,[49] the public power will lose its political character. Political power, properly so called, is merely the organized power of one class for oppressing another. If the proletariat during its contest with the bourgeoisie is compelled, by the force of circumstances, to organize itself as a class, if, by means of a revolution, it makes itself the ruling class, and, as such, sweeps away by force the old conditions of production, then it will, along with these conditions, have swept away the conditions for the existence of class antagonisms and of classes generally, and will thereby have abolished its own supremacy as a class.

In place of the old bourgeois society, with its classes and class antagonisms, we shall have an association, in which the free development of each is the condition for the free development of all.

---

[48] In the editions of 1848, point 9 reads: 'Combination of agriculture with industry, promotion of the gradual elimination of the contradictions between town and countryside'. In subsequent German editions the word 'contradictions' was replaced by 'distinctions'.

[49] The German editions have 'associated individuals' instead of 'a vast association of the whole nation'.

III Socialist and Communist Literature
1. Reactionary Socialism

a. Feudal Socialism. Owing to their historical position, it became the vocation of the aristocracies of France and England to write pamphlets against modern bourgeois society. In the French revolution of July 1830, and in the English reform agitation, these aristocracies again succumbed to the hateful upstart. Thenceforth, a serious political contest was altogether out of question. A literary battle alone remained possible. But even in the domain of literature the old cries of the restoration period* had become impossible.

In order to arouse sympathy, the aristocracy were obliged to lose sight, apparently, of their own interests, and to formulate their indictment against the bourgeoisie in the interest of the exploited working class alone. Thus the aristocracy took their revenge by singing lampoons on their new master, and whispering in his ears sinister prophecies of coming catastrophe.[50]

In this way arose feudal Socialism; half lamentation, half lampoon; half echo of the past, half menace of the future; at times, by its bitter, witty and incisive criticism, striking the bourgeoisie to the very heart's core; but always ludicrous in its effect, through total incapacity to comprehend the march of modern history.

The aristocracy, in order to rally the people to them, waved the proletarian alms-bag in front for a banner. But the people, so often as it joined them, saw on their hindquarters the old feudal coats of arms, and deserted with loud and irreverent laughter.

One section of the French Legitimists and 'Young England' exhibited this spectacle.

In pointing out that their mode of exploitation was different to that of the bourgeoisie, the feudalists forget that they exploited under circumstances and conditions that were quite different, and that are now antiquated. In showing that, under their rule, the modern

---

* Not the English Restoration 1660 to 1689, but the French Restoration 1814 to 1830. [Note by Engels to the English edition of 1888.]

---

[50] In the German editions the end of this sentence reads: 'and whispering in his ears more or less sinister prophecies'.

proletariat never existed, they forget that the modern bourgeoisie is the necessary offspring of their own form of society.

For the rest, so little do they conceal the reactionary character of their criticism that their chief accusation against the bourgeoisie amounts to this, that under the bourgeois regime a class is being developed, which is destined to cut up root and branch the old order of society.

What they upbraid the bourgeoisie with is not so much that it creates a proletariat, as that it creates a *revolutionary* proletariat.

In political practice, therefore, they join in all coercive measures against the working class; and in ordinary life, despite their highfalutin phrases, they stoop to pick up the golden apples dropped from the tree of industry,[51] and to barter truth, love, and honour for traffic in wool, beetroot-sugar, and potato spirits.*

As the parson has ever gone hand in hand with the landlord,[52] so has Clerical Socialism with Feudal Socialism.

Nothing is easier than to give Christian asceticism a Socialist tinge. Has not Christianity declaimed against private property, against marriage, against the State? Has it not preached in the place of these, charity and poverty, celibacy and mortification of the flesh, monastic life and Mother Church? Christian[53] Socialism is but the holy water with which the priest consecrates the heart-burnings of the aristocrat.

---

* This applies chiefly to Germany where the landed aristocracy and squirearchy have large portions of their estates cultivated for their own account by stewards, and are, moreover, extensive beetroot-sugar manufacturers and distillers of potato spirits. The wealthier British aristocracy are, as yet, rather above that; but they, too, know how to make up for declining rents by lending their names to floaters of more or less shady joint-stock companies. [Note by Engels to the English edition of 1888.]

51 The words 'dropped from the tree of industry' were added in the English edition of 1888.
52 The German editions have here 'feudal lord'.
53 The German editions of 1848 have 'holy' instead of 'Christian' (the texts of these editions contain an obvious misprint: 'heutige'– of today – for 'heilige'– holy).

b. Petty-Bourgeois Socialism. The feudal aristocracy was not the only class that was ruined by the bourgeoisie, not the only class whose conditions of existence pined and perished in the atmosphere of modern bourgeois society. The medieval burgesses and the small peasant proprietors were the precursors of the modern bourgeoisie. In those countries which are but little developed, industrially and commercially, these two classes still vegetate[54] side by side with the rising bourgeoisie.

In countries where modern civilization has become fully developed, a new class of petty bourgeois has been formed, fluctuating between proletariat and bourgeoisie and ever renewing itself as a supplementary part of bourgeois society. The individual members of this class, however, are being constantly hurled down into the proletariat by the action of competition, and, as modern industry develops, they even see the moment approaching when they will completely disappear as an independent section of modern society, to be replaced, in manufactures, agriculture and commerce, by overlookers, bailiffs and shopmen.

In countries like France, where the peasants constitute far more than half of the population, it was natural that writers who sided with the proletariat against the bourgeoisie, should use, in their criticism of the bourgeois regime, the standard of the peasant and petty bourgeois, and from the standpoint of these intermediate classes[55] should take up the cudgels for the working class. Thus arose petty-bourgeois Socialism. Sismondi was the head of this school, not only in France but also in England.

This school of Socialism dissected with great acuteness the contradictions in the conditions of modern production. It laid bare the hypocritical apologies of economists. It proved, incontrovertibly, the disastrous effects of machinery and division of labour; the concentration of capital and land in a few hands; over-production and crises; it pointed out the inevitable ruin of the petty bourgeois and peasant, the misery of the proletariat, the anarchy in production, the crying

---

[54] The German editions have 'this class still vegetates' instead of 'these two classes still vegetate'.

[55] The German editions have 'the petty bourgeoisie' instead of 'these intermediate classes'.

inequalities in the distribution of wealth, the industrial war of extermination between nations, the dissolution of old moral bonds, of the
old family relations, of the old nationalities.

In its positive aims, however, this form of Socialism aspires either to restoring the old means of production and of exchange, and
with them the old property relations, and the old society, or to cramp-
ing the modern means of production and of exchange, within the
framework of the old property relations that have been, and were
bound to be, exploded by those means. In either case, it is both reactionary and Utopian.

Its last words are: corporate guilds for manufacture; patriarchal
relations in agriculture.

Ultimately, when stubborn historical facts had dispersed all in-
toxicating effects of self-deception, this form of Socialism ended in a
miserable fit of the blues.[56]

c. German, or 'True', Socialism. The Socialist and Communist literature of France, a literature that originated under the pressure of a
bourgeoisie in power, and that was the expression of the struggle
against this power, was introduced into Germany at a time when the
bourgeoisie, in that country, had just begun its contest with feudal
absolutism.

German philosophers, would-be philosophers, and *beaux es-
prits,*[57] eagerly seized on this literature, only forgetting, that when these
writings immigrated from France into Germany, French social conditions had not immigrated along with them. In contact with German social conditions, this French literature lost all its immediate
practical significance, and assumed a purely literary aspect.[58] Thus,
to the German philosophers of the Eighteenth Century, the demands

---

[56] In the German editions this sentence reads: 'In its further development this trend
ended in a cowardly fit of the blues.'

[57] In the German editions the beginning of this sentence reads: 'German philosophers, semi-philosophers and lovers of fine phrases'.

[58] In the German editions of 1848 there follows: 'It must have appeared as idle
speculation on true society, on the realization of humanity.' In subsequent German editions the words 'on true society' were omitted.

of the first French Revolution were nothing more than the demands of 'Practical Reason' in general, and the utterance of the will of the revolutionary French bourgeoisie signified in their eyes the laws of pure Will, of Will as it was bound to be, of true human Will generally.

The work of the German *literati* consisted solely in bringing the new French ideas into harmony with their ancient philosophical conscience, or rather, in annexing the French ideas without deserting their own philosophic point of view.

This annexation took place in the same way in which a foreign language is appropriated, namely, by translation.

It is well known how the monks wrote silly lives of Catholic Saints *over* the manuscripts on which the classical works of ancient heathendom had been written. The German *literati* reversed this process with the profane French literature. They wrote their philosophical nonsense beneath the French original. For instance, beneath the French criticism of the economic functions of money, they wrote 'Alienation of Humanity', and beneath the French criticism of the bourgeois State they wrote, 'Dethronement of the Category of the General', and so forth.[59]

The introduction of these philosophical phrases at the back of the French historical criticisms[60] they dubbed 'Philosophy of Action', 'True Socialism', 'German Science of Socialism', 'Philosophical Foundation of Socialism', and so on.

The French Socialist and Communist literature was thus completely emasculated. And, since it ceased in the hands of the German to express the struggle of one class with the other, he felt conscious of having overcome 'French one-sidedness' and of representing, not true requirements, but the requirements of Truth; not the interests of the proletariat, but the interests of Human Nature, of Man in general, who belongs to no class, has no reality, who exists only in the misty realm of philosophical fantasy.

---

[59] In the German editions this sentence reads: 'For instance, beneath the French criticism of money relations they wrote, "Alienation of Humanity", and beneath the French criticism of the bourgeois State they wrote, "elimination of the domination of the abstractly General", etc.'

[60] The German editions have 'French theories' instead of 'French historical criticisms'.

This German Socialism, which took its schoolboy task so seriously and solemnly, and extolled its poor stock-in-trade in such mountebank fashion, meanwhile gradually lost its pedantic innocence.

The fight of the German, and, especially, of the Prussian bourgeoisie, against feudal aristocracy and absolute monarchy, in other words, the liberal movement, became more earnest.

By this, the long wished-for opportunity was offered to 'True' Socialism of confronting the political movement with the Socialist demands, of hurling the traditional anathemas against liberalism, against representative government, against bourgeois competition, bourgeois freedom of the press, bourgeois legislation, bourgeois liberty and equality, and of preaching to the masses that they had nothing to gain, and everything to lose, by this bourgeois movement. German Socialism forgot, in the nick of time, that the French criticism, whose silly echo it was, presupposed the existence of modern bourgeois society, with its corresponding economic[61] conditions of existence, and the political constitution adapted thereto, the very things whose attainment was the object of the pending struggle in Germany.

To the absolute governments,[62] with their following of parsons, professors, country squires and officials, it served as a welcome scarecrow against the threatening bourgeoisie.

It was a sweet finish after the bitter pills of floggings and bullets with which these same governments, just at that time,[63] dosed the German working-class risings.

While this 'True' Socialism thus served the governments as a weapon for fighting the German bourgeoisie, it, at the same time, directly represented a reactionary interest, the interest of the German Philistines. In Germany the *petty-bourgeois* class, a relic of the sixteenth century, and since then constantly cropping up again under various forms, is the real social basis of the existing state of things.

To preserve this class is to preserve the existing state of things in Germany. The industrial and political supremacy of the bourgeoisie

---

[61] The German editions have 'material' instead of 'economic'.

[62] The German editions have 'To the German absolute governments'.

[63] The words 'just at that time' were added in the English edition of 1888.

threatens it with certain destruction; on the one hand, from the concentration of capital; on the other, from the rise of a revolutionary proletariat. 'True' Socialism appeared to kill these two birds with one stone. It spread like an epidemic.

The robe of speculative cobwebs, embroidered with flowers of rhetoric, steeped in the dew of sickly sentiment, this transcendental robe in which the German Socialists wrapped their sorry 'eternal truths', all skin and bone, served to wonderfully increase the sale of their goods amongst such a public.

And on its part, German Socialism recognized, more and more, its own calling as the bombastic representative of the petty-bourgeois Philistine.

It proclaimed the German nation to be the model nation, and the German petty Philistine to be the typical man. To every villainous meanness of this model man it gave a hidden, higher, Socialistic interpretation, the exact contrary of its real character. It went to the extreme length of directly opposing the 'brutally destructive' tendency of Communism, and of proclaiming its supreme and impartial contempt of all class struggles. With very few exceptions, all the so-called Socialist and Communist publications that now (1847) circulate in Germany belong to the domain of this foul and enervating literature.*

2. Conservative, or Bourgeois, Socialism

A part of the bourgeoisie is desirous of redressing social grievances, in order to secure the continued existence of bourgeois society.

To this section belong economists, philanthropists, humanitarians, improvers of the condition of the working class, organizers of charity, members of societies for the prevention of cruelty to animals, temperance fanatics, hole-and-corner reformers of every imaginable kind. This form of Socialism has, moreover, been worked out into complete systems.

---

* The revolutionary storm of 1848 swept away this whole shabby tendency and cured its protagonists of the desire to dabble further in Socialism. The chief representative and classical type of this tendency is Herr Karl Grun. [Note by Engels to the German edition of 1890.]

We may cite Proudhon's *Philosophie de la Misere* as an example of this form.

The Socialistic bourgeois want all the advantages of modern social conditions[64] without the struggles and dangers necessarily resulting therefrom. They desire the existing state of society minus its revolutionary and disintegrating elements. They wish for a bourgeoisie without a proletariat. The bourgeoisie naturally conceives the world in which it is supreme to be the best; and bourgeois Socialism develops this comfortable conception into various more or less complete systems.[65] In requiring the proletariat to carry out such a system, and thereby to march straightway into the social[66] New Jerusalem, it but requires in reality, that the proletariat should remain within the bounds of existing society, but should cast away all its hateful ideas concerning the bourgeoisie.

A second and more practical, but less systematic, form of this Socialism sought to depreciate every revolutionary movement in the eyes of the working class, by showing that no mere political reform, but only a change in the material conditions of existence, in economical relations, could be of any advantage to them. By changes in the material conditions of existence, this form of Socialism, however, by no means understands abolition of the bourgeois relations of production, an abolition that can be effected only by a revolution, but administrative reforms, based on the continued existence of these relations; reforms, therefore, that in no respect affect the relations between capital and labour, but, at the best, lessen the cost, and simplify the administrative work, of bourgeois government.

Bourgeois Socialism attains adequate expression, when, and only when, it becomes a mere figure of speech.

Free trade: for the benefit of the working class. Protective duties: for the benefit of the working class. Prison Reform:[67] for the benefit of the working class. This is the last word and the only seriously meant word of bourgeois Socialism.

---

[64] The German editions have: 'want the living conditions of modern society'.

[65] The German editions have here: 'a more or less complete system'.

[66] This word was added in the English edition of 1888.

[67] The German editions have here: 'Solitary confinement'.

It is summed up in the phrase: the bourgeois is a bourgeois – for the benefit of the working class.

3. Critical-Utopian Socialism and Communism

We do not here refer to that literature which, in every great modern revolution, has always given voice to the demands of the proletariat, such as the writings of Babeuf and others.

The first direct attempts of the proletariat to attain its own ends, made in times of universal excitement, when feudal society was being overthrown, these attempts necessarily failed, owing to the then undeveloped state of the proletariat, as well as to the absence of the economic conditions for its emancipation, conditions that had yet to be produced, and could be produced by the impending bourgeois epoch alone. [68] The revolutionary literature that accompanied these first movements of the proletariat had necessarily a reactionary character. It inculcated universal asceticism and social levelling in its crudest form.

The Socialist and Communist systems properly so called, those of Saint-Simon, Fourier, Owen and others, spring into existence in the early undeveloped period, described above, of the struggle between proletariat and bourgeoisie (see Section I, Bourgeois and Proletarians).

The founders of these systems see, indeed, the class antagonisms, as well as the action of the decomposing elements in the prevailing form of society. But the proletariat, as yet in its infancy,[69] offers to them the spectacle of a class without any historical initiative or any independent political movement.

Since the development of class antagonism keeps even pace with the development of industry, the economic situation, as they find it, does not as yet offer to them the material conditions for the emancipation of the proletariat. They therefore search after a new social

---

[68] The German editions have 'material conditions' instead of 'economic conditions', and the end of the sentence is: 'and could be only the product of the bourgeois epoch'.

[69] The words 'as yet in its infancy' were added in the English edition of 1888.

science, after new[70] social laws, that are to create these conditions.

Historical[71] action is to yield to their personal inventive action, historically created conditions of emancipation to fantastic ones, and the gradual, spontaneous[72] class organization of the proletariat to an organization of society specially contrived by these inventors. Future history resolves itself, in their eyes, into the propaganda and the practical carrying out of their social plans.

In the formation of their plans they are conscious of caring chiefly for the interests of the working class, as being the most suffering class. Only from the point of view of being the most suffering class does the proletariat exist for them.

The undeveloped state of the class struggle, as well as their own surroundings, causes Socialists of this kind to consider themselves far superior to all class antagonisms. They want to improve the condition of every member of society, even that of the most favoured. Hence, they habitually appeal to society at large, without distinction of class; nay, by preference, to the ruling class. For how can people, when once they understand their system, fail to see in it the best possible plan of the best possible state of society?

Hence, they reject all political, and especially all revolutionary, action; they wish to attain their ends by peaceful means, and endeavour, by small experiments, necessarily doomed to failure, and by the force of example, to pave the way for the new social Gospel.

Such fantastic pictures of future society, painted at a time when the proletariat is still in a very undeveloped state and has but a fantastic conception of its own position, correspond with the first instinctive yearnings of that class for a general reconstruction of society.

But these Socialist and Communist publications contain also a critical element. They attack every principle of existing society. Hence they are full of the most valuable materials for the enlightenment of the working class. The practical measures proposed in them – such as the abolition of the distinction between town and country, of the family, of the carrying on of industries for the account of private

---

[70] In both cases the word 'new' was added in the English edition of 1888.

[71] The German editions have 'Social' instead of 'Historical'.

[72] The word 'spontaneous' was added in the English edition of 1888.

individuals,[73] and of the wage system, the proclamation of social harmony, the conversion of the functions of the State into a mere superintendence of production, all these proposals point solely to the disappearance of class antagonisms which were, at that time, only just cropping up, and which, in these publications, are recognized in their earliest indistinct and undefined forms only. These proposals, therefore, are of a purely Utopian character.

The significance of Critical–Utopian Socialism and Communism bears an inverse relation to historical development. In proportion as the modern[74] class struggle develops and takes definite shape, this fantastic standing apart from the contest, these fantastic attacks on it, lose all practical value and all theoretical justification. Therefore, although the originators of these systems were, in many respects, revolutionary, their disciples have, in every case, formed mere reactionary sects. They hold fast by the original views of their masters, in opposition to the progressive historical development of the proletariat. They, therefore, endeavour, and that consistently, to deaden the class struggle and to reconcile the class antagonisms. They still dream of experimental realization of their social Utopias, of founding isolated 'phalansteres', of establishing 'Home Colonies', of setting up a 'Little Icaria'* – duodecimo editions of the New Jerusalem – and to realize all these castles in the air, they are compelled to appeal to the feelings and purses of the bourgeois. By degrees they sink into the category of the reactionary [or][75] conservative Socialists depicted above, differing from these only by more systematic pedantry, and by their fanati-

---

* *Phalansteres* were Socialist colonies on the plan of Charles Fourier; *Icaria* was the name given by Cabet to his Utopia and, later on, to his American Communist colony. [Note by Engels to the English edition of 1888.]

    'Home Colonies' were what Owen called his Communist model societies. *Phalansteres* was the name of the public palaces planned by Fourier. *Icaria* was the name given to the Utopian land of fancy, whose Communist institutions Cabet portrayed. [Note by Engels to the German edition of 1890.]

---

[73] In the German editions the beginning of this sentence reads as follows: 'Their positive propositions concerning the future society, for example, abolition of the contradiction between town and country, of the family, of private profit...'.

[74] This word was added in the English edition of 1888.

[75] In the English edition of 1888 the word 'or' is omitted, but it is given in all other authorized editions.

cal and superstitious belief[76] in the miraculous effects of their social science.

They, therefore, violently oppose all political action on the part of the working class; such action, according to them, can only result from blind unbelief in the new Gospel.

The Owenites in England, and the Fourierists in France, respectively oppose the Chartists and the *Reformistes*.

VI Position of the Communists in Relation to the Various Existing Opposition Parties

Section II has made clear the relations of the Communists to the existing working-class parties, such as the Chartists in England and the Agrarian Reformers in America.

The Communists fight for the attainment of the immediate aims, for the enforcement of the momentary interests of the working class; but in the movement of the present, they also represent and take care of[77] the future of that movement. In France the Communists ally themselves with the Social-Democrats,* against the conservative and radical bourgeoisie, reserving, however, the right to take up a critical position in regard to phrases and illusions traditionally handed down from the great Revolution.

In Switzerland they support the Radicals, without losing sight of the fact that this party consists of antagonistic elements, partly of Democratic Socialists, in the French sense, partly of radical bourgeois.

In Poland they support the party that insists on an agrarian

---

* The party then represented in Parliament by Ledru-Rollin, in literature by Louis Blanc, in the daily press by the *Reforme*. The name of Social-Democracy signified, with these its inventors, a section of the Democratic or Republican party more or less tinged with Socialism. [Note by Engels to the English edition of 1888.]

The party in France which at that time called itself Socialist-Democratic was represented in political life by Ledru-Rollin and in literature by Louis Blanc; thus it differed immeasurably from present-day German Social-Democracy. [Note by Engels to the German edition of 1890.]

---

[76] The German editions have 'fanatical superstition'.

[77] The words 'and take care of' were added in the English edition of 1888.

revolution as the prime condition for national emancipation, that party which fomented the insurrection of Cracow in 1846.

In Germany they fight with the bourgeoisie whenever it acts in a revolutionary way, against the absolute monarchy, the feudal squirearchy, and the petty bourgeoisie.[78]

But they never cease, for a single instant, to instil into the working class the clearest possible recognition of the hostile antagonism between bourgeoisie and proletariat, in order that the German workers may straightway use, as so many weapons against the bourgeoisie, the social and political conditions that the bourgeoisie must necessarily introduce along with its supremacy, and in order that, after the fall of the reactionary classes in Germany, the fight against the bourgeoisie itself may immediately begin.

The Communists turn their attention chiefly to Germany, because that country is on the eve of a bourgeois revolution that is bound to be carried out under more advanced conditions of European civilization, and with a much more developed proletariat, than that of England was in the seventeenth, and of France in the eighteenth century, and because the bourgeois revolution in Germany will be but the prelude to an immediately following proletarian revolution.

In short, the Communists everywhere support every revolutionary movement against the existing social and political order of things.

In all these movements they bring to the front, as the leading question in each, the property question, no matter what its degree of development at the time.

Finally, they labour everywhere for the union and agreement of the democratic parties of all countries.

The Communists disdain to conceal their views and aims. They openly declare that their ends can be attained only by the forcible overthrow of all existing social conditions. Let the ruling classes tremble at a Communistic revolution. The proletarians have nothing to lose but their chains. They have a world to win.

WORKING MEN OF ALL COUNTRIES, UNITE!

---

[78] In the German editions the end of this sentence reads: 'against the absolute monarchy, the feudal landowners and philistinism [Kleinburgerei]'.

Frederick Engels

Preface to the English Edition of 1888

The 'Manifesto' was

published as the platform of the 'Communist League', a working-men's association, first exclusively German, later on international, and, under the political conditions of the Continent before 1848, unavoidably a secret society. At a Congress of the League, held in London in November 1847, Marx and Engels were commissioned to prepare for publication a complete theoretical and practical party programme. Drawn up in German, in January, 1848, the manuscript was sent to the printer in London a few weeks before the French revolution of February 24th. A French translation was brought out in Paris, shortly before the insurrection of June, 1848. The first English translation, by Miss Helen Macfarlane, appeared in George Julian Harney's

Red Republican, London, 1850. A Danish and a Polish edition had also been published.

The defeat of the Parisian insurrection of June, 1848, – the first great battle between Proletariat and Bourgeoisie – drove again into the background, for a time, the social and political aspirations of the European working-class. Thenceforth, the struggle for supremacy was again, as it had been before the revolution of February, solely between different sections of the propertied class; the working class was reduced to a fight for political elbow-room, and to the position of extreme wing of the Middle-class Radicals. Wherever independent proletarian movements continued to show signs of life, they were ruthlessly hunted down. Thus the Prussian police hunted out the Central Board of the Communist League, then located in Cologne. The members were arrested, and, after eighteen months' imprisonment, they were tried in October, 1852. This celebrated 'Cologne Communist trial' lasted from October 4th till November 12th; seven of the prisoners were sentenced to terms of imprisonment in a fortress, varying from three to six years. Immediately after the sentence, the League was formally dissolved by the remaining members. As to the 'Manifesto', it seemed thenceforth to be doomed to oblivion.

When the European working-class had recovered sufficient strength for another attack on the ruling classes, the International Working Men's Association sprang up. But this association, formed with the express aim of welding into one body the whole militant proletariat of Europe and America, could not at once proclaim the principles laid down in the 'Manifesto'. The International was bound to have a programme broad enough to be acceptable to the English Trades' Unions, to the followers of Proudhon in France, Belgium, Italy, and Spain, and to the Lassalleans* in Germany. Marx, who drew up this programme to the satisfaction of all parties, entirely trusted to the intellectual development of the working-class, which was sure to result from combined action and mutual discussion. The very events

---

* Lassalle personally, to us, always acknowledged himself to be a disciple of Marx, and, as such, stood on the ground of the 'Manifesto'. But in his public agitation, 1862–64, he did not go beyond demanding co-operative workshops supported by State credit. [Note by Engels.]

and vicissitudes of the struggle against Capital, the defeats even more than the victories, could not help bringing home to men's minds the insufficiency of their various favourite nostrums, and preparing the way for a more complete insight into the true conditions of working-class emancipation. And Marx was right. The International, on its breaking up in 1874, left the workers quite different men from what it had found them in 1864. Proudhonism in France, Lassalleanism in Germany were dying out, and even the Conservative English Trades' Unions, though most of them had long since severed their connection with the International, were gradually advancing towards that point at which, last year at Swansea, their President could say in their name, 'Continental Socialism has lost its terrors for us.' In fact: the principles of the 'Manifesto' had made considerable headway among the working men of all countries.

The 'Manifesto' itself thus came to the front again. The German text had been, since 1850, reprinted several times in Switzerland, England and America. In 1872, it was translated into English in New York, where the translation was published in *Woodhull and Claflin's Weekly*. From this English version, a French one was made in *Le Socialiste* of New York. Since then at least two more English translations, more or less mutilated, have been brought out in America, and one of them has been reprinted in England. The first Russian translation, made by Bakunin, was published at Herzen's *Kolokol* office in Geneva, about 1863; a second one, by the heroic Vera Zasulich,[1] also in Geneva, 1882. A new Danish edition is to be found in *Social-demokratisk Bibliothek*, Copenhagen, 1885; a fresh French translation in *Le Socialiste*, Paris, 1885. From this latter a Spanish version was prepared and published in Madrid, 1886. The German reprints are not to be counted, there have been twelve altogether at the least. An Armenian translation, which was to be published in Constantinople some months ago, did not see the light, I am told, because the publisher was afraid of bringing out a book with the name of Marx on it,

---

[1] Later on Engels himself rightly pointed out in the afterword to the article 'Social Relations in Russia', published in *Internationales aus dem Volksstaat (1871–75)*, Berlin, 1894, that the actual translator was G. V. Plekhanov.

while the translator declined to call it his own production. Of further translations into other languages I have heard, but have not seen them. Thus the history of the 'Manifesto' reflects, to a great extent, the history of the modern working-class movement; at present it is undoubtedly the most widespread, the most international production of all Socialist Literature, the common platform acknowledged by millions of working men from Siberia to California.

Yet, when it was written, we could not have called it a *Socialist* Manifesto. By Socialists, in 1847, were understood, on the one hand, the adherents of the various Utopian systems: Owenites in England, Fourierists in France, both of them already reduced to the position of mere sects, and gradually dying out; on the other hand, the most multifarious social quacks, who, by all manners of tinkering, professed to redress, without any danger to capital and profit, all sorts of social grievances; in both cases men outside the working-class movement, and looking rather to the 'educated' classes for support. Whatever portion of the working class had become convinced of the insufficiency of mere political revolutions, and had proclaimed the necessity of a total social change, that portion, then, called itself Communist. It was a crude, rough-hewn, purely instinctive sort of Communism; still, it touched the cardinal point and was powerful enough amongst the working class to produce the Utopian Communism, in France, of Cabet, and in Germany, of Weitling. Thus, Socialism was, in 1847, a middle-class movement, Communism a working-class movement. Socialism was, on the Continent at least, 'respectable'; Communism was the very opposite. And as our notion, from the very beginning, was that 'the emancipation of the working class must be the act of the working class itself,' there could be no doubt as to which of the two names we must take. Moreover, we have, ever since, been far from repudiating it.

The 'Manifesto' being our joint production, I consider myself bound to state that the fundamental proposition which forms its nucleus, belongs to Marx. That proposition is: that in every historical epoch, the prevailing mode of economic production and exchange, and the social organization necessarily following from it, form the basis upon which is built up, and from which alone can be explained, the political and intellectual history of that epoch; that consequently the whole history of mankind (since the dissolution of primitive tribal society, holding land in common ownership) has been a history of class struggles, contests between exploiting and exploited, ruling and oppressed classes; that the history of these class struggles forms a series of evolutions in which, nowadays, a stage has been reached where the exploited and oppressed class – the proletariat – cannot attain its emancipation from the sway of the exploiting and ruling class – the bourgeoisie – without, at the same time, and once and for all, emancipating society at large from all exploitation, oppression, class distinctions and class struggles.

This proposition which, in my opinion, is destined to do for history what Darwin's theory has done for biology, we, both of us, had been gradually approaching for some years before 1845. How far I had independently progressed towards it, is best shown by my *Condition of the Working Class in England.** But when I again met Marx at Brussels, in spring, 1845, he had it ready worked out, and put it before me, in terms almost as clear as those in which I have stated it here.

From our joint preface to the German edition of 1872, I quote the following:

However much the state of things may have altered during the last twenty-five years, the general principles laid down in this Manifesto are, on the whole, as correct today as ever. Here and there some detail might be improved. The practical application of the principles will depend, as the Manifesto itself states, everywhere and at all times, on the historical conditions for the time being existing, and, for that reason, no special stress is laid on the revolutionary measures proposed at the end of Section II. That passage would, in many respects, be very differently worded today. In view of the gigantic strides of Modern Industry since 1848, and of the accompanying improved and extended organization

---

* *The Condition of the Working Class in England in 1844.* By Frederick Engels. Translated by Florence K. Wischnewetzky, New York, Lovell-London. W. Reeves. 1888. [Note by Engels.]

of the working class,[2] in view of the practical experience gained, first in the February revolution, and then, still more, in the Paris Commune, where the proletariat for the first time held political power for two whole months, this programme has in some details become antiquated. One thing especially was proved by the Commune, viz., that 'the working class cannot simply lay hold of the ready-made State machinery, and wield it for its own purposes'. (*The Civil War in France; Address of the General Council of the International Working-men's Association*, London, Truelove, 1871, p.15, where this point is further developed.[3]) Further, it is self-evident, that the criticism of Socialist literature is deficient in relation to the present time, because it comes down only to 1847; also, that the remarks on the relation of the Communists to the various opposition parties (Section IV), although in principle still correct, yet in practice are antiquated, because the political situation has been entirely changed, and the progress of history has swept from off the earth the greater portion of the political parties there enumerated.

But then, the Manifesto has become a historical document which we have no longer any right to alter.

The present translation is by Mr Samuel Moore, the translator of the greater portion of Marx's *Capital*. We have revised it in common, and I have added a few notes explanatory of historical allusions.

London, 30th January, 1888

---

[2] The original German has 'in the last twenty-five years' in place of 'since 1848', and 'extended party organization' in place of 'extended organization'.
[3] *Collected Works*, 22, p. 328.

The *Manifesto* in India
A Publishing History

The story of
how *The Communist Manifesto* came to be available in Indian languages is not well-known. The Communist Party of India was founded on 17 October 1920 at Tashkent, and Communist groups were working in different centres in India from the early 1920s. The access to the *Manifesto* for Indian revolutionaries was mainly through the copies of the English editions which were smuggled into the country.

In 1922, Ranchhoddas Bhuvan Lotwala brought out a series of pamphlets on scientific socialism under the imprint of Liberty Publications. Among them was the *Manifesto*. This was the first ever printing of the document in India. It was priced 6 annas. According to S.A. Dange, founder of the Communist group in Bombay, a dozen pamphlets were brought out by Lotwala. Other booklets published in this series were *Wage, Labour and Capital* by Engels, *Religion of Capital* by Lafargue, and *Communism* by R. Palme Dutt. The March 1923 issue of the *The Socialist*, a monthly edited by Dange, advertised these pamphlets.[1] According to G. Adhikari, 'These pamphlets were among the meagre sources of knowledge of scientific socialism available to the English-educated intellectuals of those days'.[2]

The publisher of the first edition of the *Manifesto*, R.B. Lotwala, was a patriotic businessman who was attracted to Dange after reading his *Gandhi vs Lenin* published in 1921. In December 1922, he started the Lotwala Trust for advancing socialism in India.[3] He went to England in 1923 where he met left-wing Labour leaders and must have acquired some of the Marxist literature that he subsequently published. He owned the Hindustan Press which was used for printing these pamphlets and books.[4]

Bengali

The first version of the *Manifesto* published in an Indian language was in Bengali. It was translated by Soumyendranath Tagore, and published in *Ganavani* ('Voice of the People'), the weekly paper of the Workers' and Peasants' Party of Bengal edited by Muzaffar Ahmad, the founder of the first Communist group in Bengal. The *Manifesto* appeared in six issues of *Ganavani* between 12 August 1926 and 21 July 1927.[5]

Soumyendranath left for Europe in May 1927 and reached Germany in June. The last two instalments of the translation were sent by

[1] *Documents of the History of the Communist Party*, volume 2, 1923–25; edited by G. Adhikari, New Delhi 1974, p. 191

[2] Ibid., p. 193

[3] Mahadev Saha, Explanatory Notes, *Communism in India: Unpublished Documents from the National Archives of India (1919–1924)*, compiled and edited by Subodh Roy, Calcutta 1971, p. 373

[4] Ibid., p. 322

[5] The six issues of *Ganawani* which carried the *Manifesto* are: volume 1, nos. 1 (12 August 1926), 2 (19 August), 3 (26 August), 4 (2 September), 22 (14 July 1927), 23 (21 July).

him from Germany. There is a letter intercepted by British Intelli-
gence, sent by Soumyendranath from Berlin to Muzaffar Ahmad in
Calcutta, which is available in the state archives in Calcutta. The letter, dated 14 June 1927, refers among other things to the ongoing
work of the publication of the *Manifesto*. Soumyendranath wrote:

> I am sending the translation of the remaining portion of the *Com-*
> *munist Manifesto* beginning from the second chapter. I think that
> the translation of the first chapter is already out in *Ganavani*.
> Please have it compared once. Please have the entire thing pub-
> lished in two issues. Then arrange to publish it in book form. I
> am making arrangement for money. . . . As soon as my transla-
> tion has been published in *Ganavani* please advertise that the
> *Communist Manifesto* will be out shortly in book form. This will
> be the first publication of the *Ganavani* series.

Soumyendranath's translation was published in book form in 1930,
but a copy of this publication is not available.

The first Indian translator of the *Manifesto* had an interesting
career. Soumyendranath was the grand nephew of Rabindranath
Tagore. Having acquired a degree in Economics from the Presidency
College in 1921, Soumyendranath associated himself with the Congress-led nationalist movement. Disillusioned by the experience, he
came in contact with radical Swarajists who, in Bengal, had organized
a separate political party of their own, the Labour Swaraj Party, in
November 1925. The revolutionary poet, Nazrul Islam, was one of
the founders of this party. Muzaffar Ahmad joined this party in January 1926 and it was mainly due to his political influence that the Labour
Swaraj Party was reconstituted, with a more radical programme, into
a new Peasants' and Workers' Party of Bengal in the same month.
Soumyendranath joined this party. In the second conference at the
party held in February 1927, he became its General Secretary. Subsequently, he became a member of the CPI. He left for Europe in May
1927. Soumyendranath took part in the Sixth Congress of the Communist International in Moscow in 1928, though he was not an official delegate of the CPI. He left the Communist Party in 1934, after
his return to India. He formed the Communist League which later

became the Revolutionary Communist Party of India in 1937. This Trotskyite group had very limited influence.

The second Bengali translation was done by Dr Charu Sanyal, a doctor and Congress leader of Jalpaiguri and it was published in 1933. Another translation was done by a group of scholars under the guidance of Professor Sushobhan Sarkar, noted Marxist historian. This was published by the National Book Agency (NBA) in 1944. A group of Bengali writers in Moscow approved the translation made in the NBA publication and this was published by Progress Publishers, Moscow, in 1968.

Urdu

The next Indian language in which the *Manifesto* appeared was Urdu. Close on the heels of the Bengali version which appeared in *Ganavani*, the *Al-Hilal* weekly, also published from Calcutta, published the first Urdu version. However, unlike *Ganavani* which was a left-wing paper, *Al-Hilal* was founded and edited by Maulana Abul Kalam Azad, Islamic scholar and one of the foremost leaders of the Congress-led nationalist movement.

Al-Hilal carried the first two sections of the *Manifesto* entitled 'Bourgeois and Proletarians' and 'Communists and Proletarians'. These two sections contain the main content of the *Manifesto*, while the last two sections deal with the critique of pseudo-socialisms and the tactics to be adopted by Communists in various European countries. Obviously the latter two parts were considered to be of less interest or relevance to the Urdu readership.

The two parts appeared in the 4, 11 and 18 November 1927 issues successively. The introductory note by the editor mentions that a publishing house in Germany had begun a series of publications of which two volumes have already appeared. The first volume contains the selected writings of Karl Marx along with a detailed sketch of his life. The editor says that after the Russian Revolution, Communism has become a reality and it is necessary for every country to study this doctrine not only politically but also intellectually and arrive at a correct and enlightened opinion about it. The editor states that since there is no book in Urdu that gives a correct account of this revolutionary, political, and collectivist faith, it was felt that some brief writing by Marx himself would be suitable for this purpose. For this a work by Marx has been selected for publication in *Al-Hilal*. However, neither the introductory note nor the title of the article mentions that the work concerned is *The Communist Manifesto*. The title given in *Al-Hilal* is 'Communism and its Aims' (*'Communism aur uske makasid'*).

The editor is careful to point out that the work is being published only to provide the Urdu readership with the material required; this should not be taken to imply that the editor or the journal accepts the doctrine:

> In our view Communism is the natural reaction to the bourgeois inequities of modern civilization, and just as the capitalism of modern civilization has reached an extreme, Communism too is a manifestation of the other extreme. The way to virtue and truth cannot be through these extremes, it will always be a middle path.

Apparently, the translator of this version was Abdurrazak Malihabadi, though this is not specifically stated in the weekly. Malihabadi, a close confidante of Azad, lived in Calcutta and was a prominent Congressman.

Another Urdu version was rendered by Abdul Bari who wrote under the name of 'Ishtraki Adeeb' ('communist writer'). This was published in the early thirties from Lahore.

A definitive translation was done by Ali Ashraf, a senior leader of the Communist Party from Bihar, at the instance of P.C. Joshi, the then General Secretary of the Party. It was published in 1946 by Qaumi Darul Ishaat (the branch of People's Publishing House) from Lahore.

Marathi

The next in chronological order was the Marathi version of the *Manifesto*. Gangadhar Moreshwar Adhikari, who became a prominent leader of the CPI, returned from Germany in December 1928. In March 1929, he was implicated in the Meerut Communist Conspiracy case. He translated the *Manifesto* in Meerut jail in 1930–31. It was then edited by Jagannath Adhikari and R.M. Jambhekar. This translation was published by the Kamgar Vangmaya Prasarak Mandal, Parel (Mumbai) in October 1931. The first edition had 160 pages and was priced at eight annas. It was the first of a series of Marxist books for the working class published by the Mandal, which was an organization set up by the Communist Party.

The second version of the *Manifesto* in Marathi was published in 1948 by the People's Publishing House belonging to the Communist Party of India.

Tamil

In the same month that the *Manifesto* was published in Marathi, it began to appear in serialized form in Tamil translation. Although this translation and publication appears to have been incomplete, it has an interesting history. E.V. Ramaswami (EVR), the great social reformer and leader of the non-Brahmin and Self-Respect movements in the Tamil-speaking areas of the old Madras Province, popularly known as Periyar, began to publish this serialized translation in the Self-Respect movement's weekly, *Kudi Arasu* (Republic), under the title '*Samadharma Arikkai*' ('Communist Manifesto'). The weekly published from Erode, EVR's native town, serialized the translation of Chapter I ('Bourgeois and Proletarians') in five consecutive issues beginning 4 October 1931. Although there is no mention of the name of the translator or translators, the first instalment in the series carries an introduction by EVR.

In his Introduction, EVR makes a brief reference to the history of the *Manifesto* and presents his perception of why Russia (the Soviet Union) became the first country to attempt to put Communist ideas into practice. 'However', he says,

such Communist consciousness should have taken shape in India before it did in Russia. If it has not happened here, it is because various conspiracies have taken place and because the schemers have taken great care to see that the Indian people are denied access to education, knowledge, awareness of the world and a sense of self-respect, and are kept in a barbaric state. Moreover, in the name of god and religion, a consciousness has been instilled in them that being in a condition of subjugation is the will of god and a means of salvation.

But EVR does not subscribe simply to a conspiracy theory. He discerns a larger reason behind the lack of growth of Communist consciousness:

> In other countries, one factor is considered important, the capitalist–labour (rich–poor) divide. However, in India, since the divide between the upper and lower castes is rampant and primary, this serves as a fortress for the rich–poor (capitalist) ideology. Because Communism faces double opposition here, Communist consciousness has not grown.

At the end of the fifth instalment in the translated version of Chapter I of the *Manifesto*, which appeared in the 1 November 1931 issue of *Kudi Arasu*, there is an announcement that the first Chapter is over and that the second will follow. However, the subsequent issues of the weekly do not carry the rest of the Tamil translation of the *Manifesto*. It is unlikely that the translation was completed. In fact, a month after the last instalment of Chapter I of the *Manifesto* was published, *Kudi Arasu* (issue of 13 December 1931) carried an editorial announcing that EVR was leaving that very day on a voyage to Europe. The Soviet Union was among the countries he visited. He spent six weeks there, from 14 February to 17 May 1932. It is noteworthy that this outstanding social reformer attempted to publish the *Manifesto* in Tamil and to think about its application to Indian conditions on the eve of a visit to the Soviet Union.

The first full Tamil translation of the *Manifesto* was published much later – in April 1948 – by the Janasakthi Prasuralayam, the CPI publishing house in Chennai. The translator was M. Ismat Basha who contributed a 16-page introduction to the 91-page book. '*Kammunist Katchiyin Arikkai*' (literally, 'Manifesto of the Communist Party') was priced at 12 annas (75 paise).

It is fitting that the *Manifesto* got published first in Bengali, Urdu, Marathi, and Tamil, as it is in the centres where these languages predominate that the Communist movement first struck roots. The early Communist groups were based in Calcutta, Bombay, Lahore and Madras.

Malayalam

Closely following the Tamil publication came the Malayalam version. In Kerala, Idappalli Karunakara Menon, who translated classics like *War and Peace* and *Crime and Punishment*, translated and published the *Manifesto* in 1932. This version was titled '*Samasthi Vada Vijnapanam*'. The Malayalam version appeared four years before the Communist Party was founded in Kerala.

In the early forties, E.M.S. Namboodiripad, Unni Raja and M.S. Devadas translated some important Marxist works including the *Manifesto*. In 1948, a revised edition was published in which D.M. Pottekkatt was mentioned as the translator. More editions were later published by Prabhath Books and others.

Telugu

P. Sundarayya, one of the founders of the Communist Party in Andhra Pradesh and South India, translated the *Manifesto* in Telugu in 1933. This was, however, not printed but circulated in cyclostyled form. In a report sent to the Central Committee, the Secretary of the Madras State Committee reported that this translation of the *Manifesto* was being distributed among the cadres. Interestingly, 'Principles of Communism' (by Engels) was also translated alongwith the *Manifesto*. Later, Kambhampati Satyanarayana, one of the senior Communist leaders in Andhra, translated the *Manifesto* and it was published by the Communist Party. P. Ramachandra Reddy, a well-known critic also got the *Manifesto* translated and published it. Progress Publishers, Moscow continued to reprint it.

Gujarati

The first Gujarati edition of the *Manifesto* was published in 1934 by the Navi Duniya (New World) Karyalaya Publications Centre in

Ahmedabad. The Navi Duniya Centre was the first left group in Gujarat. The Centre had two convenors, Ranchod Narayandas Patel and Dinkar Mehta. Patel had become the secretary of the first Communist group in Gujarat in December 1933. Mehta, a Joint Secretary of the All-India Congress Socialist Party, was one of founders of the Communist movement in Gujarat. Navi Duniya brought out a *Granthmala* (series of pamphlets), and the *Manifesto* was the third in the series. It was priced at 6 annas and was printed at Geeta Printers, Ahmedabad. Some of the other titles in the *Granthmala* were *Socialism: Utopian and Scientific* by Engels, *Whither Russia* by Jawaharlal Nehru, and *Changing Russia.*

The *Manifesto* was translated by Chandrabhai Bhatt, one of the pioneering Communist leaders of Gujarat. He was a prolific writer, with about 80 publications to his credit. He explained the priniciples of Communism in his works, engaged in political polemics, and wrote literary works. A notable feature of his translation is that he appended 39 notes to explain the various terms and events referred to in the text for the Gujarati readership.

Hindi

In Hindi, the distinction of being the first tranlator and publisher of the *Manifesto* goes to Ayodhya Prasad. As a Communist, he was implicated in the Meerut Conspiracy case. He translated the *Manifesto* from jail and after his release in 1933, he published it in 1934 under the imprint of the Matrubhoomi Printing Works, Jhansi. This edition was banned by the British authorities.

Oriya

In Oriya, the *Manifesto* was translated by Bhagabati Panigrahi and published under the title '*Vaigyanik samyabad*' ('Scientific Communism') in 1936 by the Congress Socialist Party. Panigrahi was one of the founders of the Communist Party in Orissa and became the first secretary of the Orissa unit of the Party. Earlier, he was the secretary of the Congress Socialist Party in Orissa. Besides being the organizer and leader of various worker–peasant movements, Bhagbati was also a noted creative writer and initiated the progressive literary movement in Oriya. He died of dysentry at the young age of 34 while doing famine-related relief work in 1943.

Punjabi

The first Punjabi edition of the *Manifesto* was published in November 1944 by the Progressive Publishers, Lahore. A second edition was brought out in 1950 by Sada Yug Publishers, Delhi. The translator was Professor Randhir Singh, the well-known Marxist political scientist. This version appeared in an improved edition from the Punjabi Book Centre Publishers, Jalandhar, in 1959.

Here we have tried to trace the history of the *Manifesto* in Indian languages up to Independence. In the fifties and later, the *Manifesto* was published regularly in different Indian languages by Progress Publishers, Moscow.

Index

Index

Index

Index

Index

Index

Index

Index

Index

SIGNPOST is a series that aims to reflect the views of the left and help create a common, progressive understanding of issues that matter.

SIGNPOST will address a wide variety of subjects. Each publication in the series shall focus on a single topic that is significant in debates of the day, in a manner that is serious, informative, analytically sound and politically interventionist. The series will aim to bring advanced knowledge to the general readers and to activists in movements for social transformation.

SIGNPOST is committed to analyses that are clearly written, attractively produced and moderately priced.

N. RAM
Riding the Nuclear Tiger

By exploding five nuclear devices on May 11 and 13, 1998 at Pokhran, the BJP-led government hijacked India's independent, peace-oriented nuclear policy and twisted it out of shape. N. Ram (Editor, *Frontline*), drawing on scientific inputs and assessments from physicist T. Jayaraman, assesses the reasons and implications of this move in a manner accessible to both the interested layperson and the specialist.

'. . . the book accurately delienates some of the basic causes and consequences of the May 1998 [nuclear] tests. . . . N. Ram has warmly acknowledged the contribution of T. Jayaraman, whose expertise is clearly discernible in the more technical parts of the book discussing post-Pokhran II claims, in particular highlighting the enormous difficulties India will have in establishing a credible "minimum deterrent" against any country other than Pakistan. . . . This call for a return to nuclear sanity can only be endorsed. '

The Hindustan Times

Demy 8vo, pp. viii + 120, hardcover Rs 175, paperback Rs 60